To Unshakable Bliss

A Techie's Adventure

By Seren   Nish

First paperback edition Jan 2024

ISBN (hardcover) 979-8-9898310-3-6

ISBN (paperback) 979-8-9898310-0-5

ISBN (ebook) 979-8-9898310-1-2

ISBN (audiobook) 979-8-9898310-2-9

Contents

Introduction

The world, a magnificent display of nature's wonders, has borne witness to remarkable feats of human talent, love, and heroic endeavors throughout the history of humanity.

Mythological folklore and other religious stories weave in frameworks for civic conduct and resilience. As children, societies introduced us to these stories, fueling our imagination, molding our ethical beliefs, and igniting inspiration.

In our youthful innocence, we dreamed big – whether to champion a cause, invent the next big thing, fight injustice, create works of art, amass wealth, fame, and so on. These ambitions awakened our sense of purpose and drove us into action.

However, over time, we began to think more deeply. As we did, the intensity of passion waned. Once as fierce as the dazzling sun, it dimmed, clouded by the fog of fear and skepticism. Then profound and unsettling questions began to surface: Who am I? What is the meaning or purpose of my life? Why is suffering so pervasive? What lies beyond death?

The search for answers to these questions is not only worthy but enriching. It adds depth and dimension to our lives, which have largely existed in the physical realm, consuming sensory pleasures and enduring worldly pains. An existence devoid of such inquiry feels incomplete.

Undoubtedly, challenges are an inevitable part of the human experience. George Orwell writes, "Most people get a fair amount of fun out of their lives, but on balance, life is suffering, and only the very young or the very foolish imagine otherwise."

This isn't to negate life's joys but to highlight the need for tools to find meaning from these sufferings.

Life's unpredictable nature means we seldom control when or how trials arise. Drawing from Marcus Aurelius, humans can be likened to a dog tethered to a moving cart. When the cart moves, the dog is moved whether it wants to or not. Its only choice is to run along the cart or get dragged. Our constantly moving world also offers us limited options: to go with its flow or get pulled along.

Throughout history, our ancestors have searched for answers to alleviate suffering, navigate its unpredictability, and find a path beyond the sensory experiences of life.

In the 6th century BCE, ancient Chinese philosopher Laozi penned his reflections on nature's intrinsic balance in the Tao Te Ching, which translates to "The Way and Its Virtues." These 81 short perceptive poems reveal the illusory nature of reality and that the infinitely good and eternal source of creation lies within all individuals.

During this global spiritually fertile period, luminaries like Vyasa and Valmiki in ancient India breathed life into monumental epics—the Mahabharata and Ramayana. These sagas emphasized righteousness and moral duty. The Bhagavad Gita, within the famous Mahabharata epic, charts pathways to divine communion through knowledge, action, devotion, and meditation.

The bedrock of yogic philosophy lies in the Upanishads[1] estimated to have been composed between 800 and 600 BCE and likely passed down orally for centuries. Their interpretations emphasize the world as unreal or 'Maya' (illusion), emphasizing that the sole eternal reality remains elusive—beyond our senses of sound, sight, touch, etc. Core practices involve meditation through mantra chanting to attain deeper states of consciousness.

Around the 5th century BCE, Buddha's teachings emerged, preaching an eightfold path to end suffering by elimination of desire. Practices like Vipassana aim to gain insight into oneself through observation of bodily sensations, feelings, and mental states without judgement.

In the subsequent era, Stoicism took root in Greece through thinkers like Socrates, Epictetus, Seneca, and others. They

---

[1] Upanishads were part of the Vedas. The Upanishads are considered to be shruti, or "that which is heard." This means there was no author of these texts, they are believed to have been revealed to the sages and teachers who composed them.

professed that inner peace comes from self-control and an alignment with the natural order.

Notably, core Stoic principles—such as the emphasis on virtue, the concept of universal brotherhood, and the acceptance of circumstances beyond one's control—found their way into the foundational teachings of Christianity.

By the Islamic Golden Age in the 8th century CE, Sufi poets in the Middle East were composing verses about intimate relationship with the Divine, achieved through love, devotion, and ego dissolution. While adhering to Islamic tenets, traditional Sufis embarked on mystic odysseys, seeking the personal experience of God through fasting, prayers, chanting (zikr), and meditation. Intriguingly, echoes of non-dualistic[2] principles from the Upanishads resonate in the teachings of some Sufi mystics.

Throughout diverse eras, geographies, and cultures, enlightened beings have tirelessly sought to codify insights into formulas for a good life. By codify, I mean systematize the principles that can reduce suffering and improve well-being into teachings and tools.

---

[2] Non-dualism, or Advaita in Sanskrit, is one of the central concepts of Upanishads. It proposes that there is only one fundamental reality and everything else is an illusion. It is not saying that God exists in everything. In fact, it is saying only God exists and nothing else does.

The timeless wisdom emphasizes minimizing attachments to fleeting sensory indulgences, prestige, wealth, and power by uncovering their impermanence. The instructions orient focus on the changeless singularity at the heart of existence. Techniques to actualize this shift involve devotion, mindfulness, and self-inquiry as mechanisms to relinquish egoic clinging.

A lucid summary of Vedic explorations can be captured by the simple declaration from the Chandogya Upanishad of the Sama Veda: "Tat tvam asi," translating as "That is Self."

Seekers across history can be broadly categorized into those seeking the divine or "That" and those seeking a deeper understanding of the "Self."

Major religions such as Islam, Christianity, Hinduism, and Judaism have traditionally focused on pursuing "That."

In contrast, Buddhists, Jains, existentialists, contemporary philosophers, and researchers have sought to gain a clearer perspective on the "Self."

Despite their distinct goals, both quests mandate comprehending the world's transiency and our limited influence over life's events. A recurring theme is the call to detach from worldly desires by mastering the body and mind. Such discipline requires discernment and practice.

Ultimately, both journeys merge into a singular truth. This convergence is beautifully articulated by the Sufi mystic Rumi: "I found God when I was seeking myself and found myself when I was seeking God."

Yet, there appear to be two distinct trails in the quest for inner peace and enduring happiness: one carved by deep devotion and steadfast faith in the divine traversed by the "That" seekers and the other sculpted by rigorous analytical reasoning and research preferred by the "Self" seekers.

In earlier eras, achieving inner peace through introspection, logic, and disciplined practice was the realm of a dedicated few. Today, with basic needs met for many, there's a broader space for delving into existential questions. Advancements in neuroscience, education, and religious freedom enable many to explore deeper facets of our existence.

Most modern minds, characterized by skepticism, demand empirical evidence of "That" and are more inclined toward practices focused on understanding and improving the "Self." Though faith in a divine power brings solace in life's chaos for many, not everyone can believe in a supernatural entity that can neither be described nor sensed.

This book ventures into the interplay of the timeless scriptures and the recent scientific findings, proposing that we bridge the chasm to faith through knowledge and reason. Embarking on any journey of introspection is not just an intellectual exploration but perhaps the most rewarding aspect of being alive.

In a twist on Plato's allegory of the cave[3], human life is compared to a puppet, its strings in the hands of the Gods. They have the power to influence our actions and control our fate. However, Socrates counters this perspective, emphasizing our possession of the 'golden cord' – our inherent ability to reason. As long as we retain and exercise this intellectual ability, a guiding light will illuminate our path, helping us navigate life's maze of deception and illusion.

It's essential that we remain steadfast in our skepticism and determination, lest we become perpetual prisoners to external forces. Yielding to the material world would render us mere servants to our body, driven solely to meet its

---

[3] Inspired by: The Great Ideas of Philosophy by Prof. Daniel N. Robison Plato's allegory of the cave describes individuals who have been chained inside a cave for their entire lives, facing a blank wall. Shadows are cast onto this wall by objects passing in front of a fire positioned behind them. Over time, these chained individuals come to recognize and interpret these shadows as their reality because it's all they have ever known. However, the philosopher among them breaks free and discovers that these shadows are mere illusions, far removed from the true nature of things. This awakening is facilitated by the "golden cord" of reason—a symbolic representation of critical thinking, enlightenment, and firm commitment to truth.The philosopher is willing to face the light, even though it is initially blinding.

demands or mere puppets controlled by the will of our emotions and at the mercy of circumstances.

So, the lingering questions are: How do we overcome these seemingly insurmountable forces of nature? How can we make the fleeting state of happiness permanent?

Every once in a while, we encounter a truly liberated soul, radiating unyielding peace despite prevailing chaos. Such individuals exhibit no traces of pride, and neither criticism nor misfortune can deter them. Their actions are untainted by desire or fear, making them unbreakable and unconquerable. This brings to mind a verse from a poem by William Ernest Henley:

> "Out of the night that covers me,
> Black as a pit from pole to pole,
> I thank whatever gods maybe,
> For my unconquerable soul.
> It matters not how strait the gate,
> How charged with punishments the scrolls,
> I am the master of my fate,
> I am the captain of my soul."

How do these liberated souls attain such unshakable inner peace? Logic and reason provide the crucially important foundational work of questioning assumptions, dismantling dogma, and analyzing life's challenges through a rational lens. This tempers reactivity and separates momentary emotions from the enduring truth.

Yet, reason alone often cannot surmount some of life's incessant grind. There comes a point where knowledge ends, and a leap of faith begins. By faith, I refer not to blind belief but rather to informed trust, like choosing to fully commit to a challenge because you judge it to be worthwhile.

My faith emerged when I sincerely yearned for solutions - complementing logic with hope, conviction, and meaning. Together, reason and faith intertwined within me to provide a compass for navigating life's stormy seas. The former grants agency, while the latter connects to forces greater than one's solitary self.

Pursued by such faith that had emerged as an eternal force inseparable from my own being, I began writing this book. And although I had never authored a book before, a story persistently tugged at my awareness, vying for expression. It molded my thoughts and guided my words.

Listening to the accounts of great sages and thinkers, I have always wondered what it would be like for a regular professional like myself to embark on a quest for bliss. What would trigger such an expedition, and what would the adventure look like? I indulged in a thought experiment of how the teachings of a variety of ancient Sanskrit scriptures when combined with philosophy and the findings of neuroscience, could be used to flesh out the tools required to live a monk-like life while being passionately engaged in it.

This fictional tale unfolds around Qayum[4] (pronounced kah.yew.oom), our protagonist, a children's book author and a former technologist seeking to find meaning in life.

In Part 1, Qayum tries to find happiness through worldly success and validation. However, transient worldly pleasures fail to provide lasting contentment. Her intense desire to find truth and meaning, along with faith in herself and in the possibilities, qualifies her as a **'Seeker.'** She practices the techniques to master her mind and body's impulses through habit formation, tempering likes/dislikes, and maintaining equanimity in life's dualities.

Part 2 finds Qayum working through the grip of past trauma, entangled in her wounded ego. Through mystical experiences, Qayum discovers tools to detach from her ego and actions' outcomes, thus progressing to the state of **'Detached.'**

---

[4] Qayum inspired by an Arabic word for 'self-reliant' and 'ever-living.' It is one of the names of Allah in Islam and is used to describe the attribute of being utterly free from dependence on anyone or anything.
In Sufism, it denotes a channel of divine grace and guidance.

Qayum becomes increasingly 'Awakened' in Part 3, with the knowledge that the world - all things, people, time, and space are impermanent and unreal.

Ultimately, in Part 4, she is transported into the uncharted realms of consciousness as the 'Absolute.' As a karma yogi, she maintains a mind clean and polished for a continuous view of 'That,' which cannot be seen.

Qayum is not alone in her transformative quest. She is guided by the love and support of those dear to her, nudged by the omnipotent forces of the universe, and led by the breadcrumbs of truth that mark her path.

As the story took shape, its purpose became clear. For decades, I had sought meaning, exploring philosophies. This book embodies my fantasy - to embark on a treasure hunt, the prize being self-realization and everlasting bliss. I imagine the adventure filled with suspense and thrill involves navigating twists, overcoming challenges, and maintaining virtue. Ultimately, when the mind is pristine and still like the calm waters of a mirror lake undisturbed by ripples, the complete self can be glimpsed.

The yearning to escape suffering's grip resonates universally. From ancient sages, continental philosophers, and modern physicists to neuroscientists, the quest for enduring contentment continues. With reverence to those who have walked this path before me, I seek to build upon their insights as I devise a course to further explore the state of 'purnam' - the Sanskrit term for complete or entire.

To commence this spiritual journey, it feels fitting to seek blessings through an ancient invocation. The 'Shanti Path' or 'Peace Invocation' from the Brihadaranyaka Upanishad (5.1) fine-tunes the mind and spirit. It mitigates conflicts and inspires stillness and a sense of wholeness in the seeker.

pūrṇamadaḥ pūrṇamidaṁ pūrṇātpūrṇamudacyate |
That is absolute, this is absolute. From that absolute comes this absolute.

pūrṇasya pūrṇamādāya pūrṇamevāvaśiṣyate ||
If absoluteness is taken away from absoluteness, only the absolute remains.

The shloka reveals that both the macrocosm (cosmic reality) and the microcosm (individual reality) are complete and whole. Both are infinite, given that infinity plus or minus infinity remains infinity.

Drawing strength from this powerful Mantra, I must now confront my vulnerability as I pour words onto the pages, exposing my private struggles and fears. I hope my words find comfort in the embrace of a reader who uses them to reflect on their individual struggles.

This story of Qayum, a Silicon Valley tech professional, has echoes of the trials faced by every human being through the eternal cycle of existence. In that sense, it has been narrated innumerable times, each version infusing the unique sensibilities of its era into this timeless journey. I must tell her story once more.

For, in the ceaseless cyclical flow of time and space - stories are reborn, and epics rediscover their voice. Perhaps, in some distant future or unfathomable dimension, I may stumble upon these very words and, in that vanishing moment, remember the person I once was - or pretended to be.

Part 1: The Seeker

Mumukṣā is the seeker filled with longing for liberation.

Chapter 1: This Too Shall Pass

The sun begins its descent toward the horizon. Some clouds are on fire with vibrant orange, crimson red, and candy yellow blended in perfection. The others further away look like coals on a kid's canvas, whose favorite colors are deep purples and dark blues. An old, noisy car huffs and puffs its way through the curves of Highway-1. Qayum is immersed in her favorite album - Savage Garden - finding a connection to her teenage self, who once was an unstoppable force of positivity.

"I want to stand with you on the mountain. I want to bathe with you in the sea," she sings into the wind, competing with the engine's loud rumble. The vivid and unreal colors of the sky appear so striking that if it were a painting, she would have critiqued the artist for the stark contrast, she muses.

Today marks the beginning of her book tour, a new chapter offering hope and promise after years of tumultuous change. Qayum's spirits soar as she embraces the joys of traveling. Exploring new places holds a special place in her heart, representing adventure, excitement, and a break from the mundane. Prakashay, her agent, has organized a few book reading and signing sessions in the coastal towns of California. Afterward, she plans to drive to San Francisco and catch a flight to Denmark for an award ceremony. Her final destination is another book reading tour in East Africa. The entire trip is three weeks long, which is the perfect length for any trip. Anything longer makes you homesick, and anything shorter just leaves you hungry for more.

"I want to lay like this forever... " She continues competing with the engine's persistent rumble. Her glance drifts to the surreal views on her left: dazzling golden waves, a sparkly hue crowning every wildflower adorning the cliffs, and everything radiating a bronze glow, including the rocks.

She yearns to linger in this moment forever. Everything is so clear, and she thinks, "I feel one with the road. I am savoring the ride." Just then, her mind involuntarily races back to the past. It's been six years since she abandoned her corporate life in product development, a decision prompted by a layoff during the previous recession. She had dedicated two decades to that career, believing it would endure until her final days.

However, the betrayal and anger she felt when cast aside left a painful sting. Her allies justified it as a financial decision by some paper pusher, while others said it was just a dice roll. It did not matter what the reason was - the agony was searing, and she found it impossible to bounce back. She could not get back on that horse ever again. She admitted defeat.

On that defining day six years ago, a metamorphic event was triggered. That morning, Qayum's login failed. She firmly believed it was a computer error. "How can this be?" she wondered aloud, "I did not change my password. Wait, I cannot access anything. What did I do?"

"We have very difficult news to share. It is with regret that we inform you that your role is impacted as we reduce our workforce. We no longer have a job for you..." read the site Qayum was redirected to after trying to log in to the corporate page.

Qayum froze, trying to evaluate if this was really happening or if she merely needed to wake up from a nightmare. She read the message again and again: "We no longer have a job for you ..."

Eventually, it sank in, and then she screamed, "Ahh! I did not finish the pictures I was building for the strategy document, and the last customer persona still needs some work. I just needed one more day. So much unfinished work needs to be wrapped up. Friends, I need to say goodbyes and thankyous to. What a terrible way to end this! I am not done yet - please, I need a little more time."

Qayum's emotions oscillated wildly those first days - soaring from enraged indignation to plunging depths of despair. She grieved as if a loved one had died. The company had been an integral part of her life for years, almost becoming an extension of her identity.

Within that misery, a palpable sense of relief emerged, like a sea breeze soothing the sticky humidity. No longer did she need to tread the corporate tightrope or suppress her passion for speedy results. She was now unshackled, ready to embark on her next adventure.

In the aftermath, work friends and colleagues inundated her with emails, messages, and calls. Their words, full of praise and disbelief, echoed like eulogies in her ears. "You were incredible; this doesn't make any sense." "You've done wonders for the team." "We'll miss you." While these sentiments provided momentary comfort, they also amplified her grief. She felt a ghost eavesdropping on her own memorial service.

Through the outpouring of support, there was a conspicuous silence. Nandan, her manager, hadn't reached out. Just a week prior, with whispers of layoffs swirling around, he had assured Qayum of her and her team's job security. "Surely, he couldn't have known? But how could he lack the basic decency to call? Then again, would his words have made a difference?" She wasn't so sure. Emotions clouded her judgment, making it hard to see clearly. It was time to move on, leaving behind the tech world she once believed was her entire universe but from where she felt so unceremoniously pushed out.

Over the subsequent years, Qayum experimented with a variety of ventures. She dove into property management, opened a specialty cafe, and took a chance on launching online tutoring services - chasing each pioneering dream with zeal. Each idea, initially shimmering with promise, ended up barely breaking even. Despite her exhaustive efforts and hiring the top-tier talent, the outcomes never met her grand visions of entrepreneurial success.

In the quiet moments between these ventures, Qayum found refuge in her writing. She reimagined age-old Eastern myths with lively narratives and sketches, losing herself in imaginary lands filled with all manners of creatures personified. When the well of ideas for innovative start-up pursuits finally ran dry, she decided to compile her writings. The result was a manuscript for a children's book.

With renewed purpose, Qayum ventured into the maze of the literary world, seeking an agent. She persevered through countless rejections until, one day, her inbox bore the message: "Hello, Qayum, I see potential in your book, and with your commitment, we can steer it to publication." The sign-off read, "Warm regards, Prakashay." The email was the spark she desperately needed to fight off the cold senselessness that constantly lurked around her in recent months.

Their first meeting took place over a video call. Prakashay, a retired gentleman with an air of confidence, had vast experience in publishing. With each harsh critique of her work, he released a warm, endearing laugh. Over numerous sessions, he imparted two virtues to her: the courage to weather criticism and the patience to let things unfold at their natural pace.

Patiently guiding her through the rewrites, he would explain the unseen iceberg lurking beneath his edits. "Publishing rewards resilience," he would say. 'For every book that ascends bestseller peaks, nine sink silently despite earnest efforts.'

He reminded her of writers who weathered endless rejections before acclaimed debuts. She clung to those flares of hope as she persevered through the many books. She had grown very fond of him.

Completely engrossed in her thoughts, Qayum drives, relying mostly on the auto-pilot section of her brain. Her attention snaps back to the road when another car appears abruptly around a sharp bend. She realizes that she missed the warning sign for the upcoming bend in the road. Fortunately, the other vehicle is moving at a slow speed, and the passing maneuver is uneventful.

As she steadies herself, the melody of "To the Moon & Back" fills the car again - the album has looped back to the first song.

At that moment, with the purple darkness swallowing the last glow from the sun, Qayum thinks to herself: "My mind is perfectly at peace right now, and I could just live my entire life in this one moment." Almost immediately, another voice within her objects, "No! I can't possibly live like this forever - eternal perfection can get so unbearably dull!"

She is pulled from her reverie by a dense fog rolling in, obscuring her vision. The sudden transformation is startling. "Why this abrupt shift? Where did the clear skies go? Is my psyche influencing the world around me?" she wonders. Every time life seems perfect, a restlessness brews within, seeking stimulation through fresh challenges. It's as if her inner self craves the volatility that disruption brings. She sees this pattern reflected in the abrupt arrival of the fog. The universe seems to mirror her own inner conflicts, hurling challenges at her to evade boredom or apathy.

As the haze descends, droplets swirl across the windshield, erased by the frantic swiping of wipers. The world beyond her car dissolves, obscured by the thickening fog. Qayum is now fully alert behind the wheel, her senses heightened to make out the road ahead. She eases her foot off the accelerator, silences the music, and focuses intently on navigating through the mist.

Just as the fog seems impenetrable, the outline of a cottage emerges—a welcoming sight. She turns into the driveway and shuts off the engine, its steady purr giving way to the quiet of the woods.

On the door, she finds a note from the hosts, "Welcome Qayum! We hope you enjoy your stay! - Andy & Joe." She checks her phone for the code to the keypad lock, punches it in, and swings the door open. A quick glance around, and she murmurs approvingly, "Oh, this will do nicely."

Heading back to the car, she opens the trunk. It's packed with boxes of her latest book and her previous bestseller. These will serve her well during her upcoming visits to schools, community centers, and libraries. She's been assured that the bookstores have stocked up for the events. A small, vibrant orange suitcase containing her essentials for the road trip is nestled between the stacks of books. Further inside, another larger black bag is prepped for her impending international journey. She retrieves only the small suitcase, deliberately leaving the rest behind.

In their college days, Qayum and Vatsal began as two individuals finding their academic rhythm together. While Qayum was captivated by theory and the intricacies of the abstract, Vatsal was always eager to roll up his sleeves and delve into the practical. This complementary dynamic made their study sessions productive and fun. As the semesters rolled by, the camaraderie rooted in mutual respect began to unfurl into deeper affection. Their shared passion for philosophy and literature meant their conversations were always animated and intellectually stimulating.

While Vatsal rapidly ascended the corporate ladder, recipient of awards, and envied promotions, Qayum contended against subtle prejudices barring her from the C-suite's old boys club dominating Silicon Valley. Over the years, ambition curdled to despair at her stunted career.

It seemed Vatsal's success also anointed him as the default advisor for family and friends. Society rewards one-dimensional success far more than balanced achievement across areas. Corporate executives are revered and consulted across unrelated domains - like the way celebrities are looked up as fashion icons or diet gurus despite their limited qualifications there.

In contrast, balancing myriad responsibilities as caregivers and homemakers involves more varied talents - yet garners far less respect. Though possessing a richer form of achievement vital to humanity, women shouldering diverse roles are seldom acknowledged.

Despite reaching the pinnacles of worldly validation, Vatsal remained ever-grounded in what truly mattered - his actions aligned with his wisdom that strength of character surpassed fame. Through Qayum's uncertainties and her career troughs, Vatsal stood like a rock, supporting and encouraging her. He cheered her along through all her failed ventures with unconditional positivity - "It's for the best," he would reassure her. Or he would say, "Something even better is waiting for you." She loved him and was grateful for this one thing that was always right in her life.

As she settles into the cottage, she spots a curated spread on the table— a bottle of wine, an assortment of pastries, and cheese thoughtfully arranged by the house's caretakers.

Surveying the outside, Qayum realizes that the fog has lifted, revealing a clear sky with a half-moon suspended upside down. For a moment, she wonders if the fog was a mere figment of her imagination or her very own creation.

She believes that people inadvertently create their own realities through their thoughts. Her proof is Sarla Aunty, a childhood neighbor who was a chronic worrier with the worst luck. She would imagine awful outcomes, and the universe seemed to go out of its way to make these unusual events happen for her. Sarla Aunty's travels would involve missed flights, lost luggage, or unexpected floods during the dry season. Her refrigerator would break down before the big dinner she was hosting, or just when her investments took a nosedive, a series of bills would appear.

These unfortunate events that happened to Sarla Aunty intrigued Qayum as she would listen to her lament her terrible luck and then catalog the other bad things that could be in store for her. Qayum wonders if her challenges over the past few years were caused by her persistent despair or boredom. Then, she recalls an old tale from her mother about how Qayum would sometimes lock horns with the wind. With a smirk, she murmurs, uncorking the wine, "I spar with nothingness too, and for a solid reason— it keeps life interesting!"

This dance with the void is her shield from the ever-present emptiness, a refuge from the loud silence of existence. Trying to keep things interesting is Qayum's way of being distracted from the dull pain of looking for purpose. Qayum finds joy when solving life's tricky puzzles or in moments of triumph, but she wonders what it would take for happiness to be a permanent resident. Why does it always seem to be evaporating?

Pouring the wine into a glass, Qayum breathes in its rich aroma. The velvety merlot's hints of oak and spice on her palette, accented by the crisp night air on her skin, induce calm. Between bites of the delectable spread, her gaze drifts upwards, scouring the heavens, hoping to spot any star willing to accompany the moon tonight.

The thought of venturing out for dinner seems unappealing. Instead, she decides to treat herself to the simple luxury of a prolonged, warm bath.

As she waits for the hot water to fill the tub, her phone rings. It is Vatsal. "How was the drive?" he says with a familiar affection. She relives the beautiful sunset, the ocean waves, and the flowering cliffs as she describes it to Vatsal. She then remembers her drifting away into thoughts and nearly missing the sharp turn but chooses not to share the incident.

25

Given her reputation at home for occasional forgetfulness or minor accidents—usually the result of her introspective trances—she'd rather not add to Vatsal's list of concerns. Besides, the fog she thought she'd seen was perhaps never there?

They continue their conversation, meandering through the details of Vatsal's workday and his upcoming business trip. He's set to fly to Chicago, then onward to New York. The highlight of their chat is his plan to rendezvous with Qayum in Copenhagen the following week for her book awards ceremony.

Their goodbyes are short and loving. Hanging up, she submerges into the bath, allowing herself to inhabit the moment without any further interruptions from her mind.

Warmed and relaxed by her bath, Qayum heads to bed.

As her eyelids grow heavy, a thought emerges to describe how the fleeting bursts of elation, purpose, and pleasures in life are like the sunsets - glorious but transient. Failing to hold on to the thought to study its purpose, she drifts into dreams, nuzzled up to the silence of the night.

Chapter 2: The Unknowable Known

In a dimension beyond the constraints of time and matter, unfathomable to human understanding, reside three guardians of age-old wisdom: Sakshi, the eternal observer; Prakruti, the expression of all laws of nature; and Maya, the master of illusions. Their voices are timeless, echoing the deepest truths of the cosmos and directed at those who yearn to understand the fundamentals of existence.

Sakshi materializes as a luminous figure, the golden sheen of her silk robe exuding the warm glow from within. Though formless, this projection allows temporary capture by mortal imagination. As the primordial source perpetuating existence, her grace can soothe any restless being.

She is seated on a cushioned chair, sipping the fragrant Sukku Malli coffee—a rich blend crafted from the choicest coffee beans, infused with the zesty notes of dry-roasted ginger and coriander seeds. Its fragrance fills the air.

From this realm, she sends forth messages, ripples in the cosmic fabric, that contain the secrets of existence itself. By her side is the enigmatic Maya, a personification of the grand illusion that manifests itself as the perceptible universe. In this haven with unparalleled beauty and tranquility, they probe together mysteries of human experience.

Sakshi is the fundamental energy animating all creation, from sprawling galaxies to the humble atom. The constraints of genesis and entropy do not apply to this timeless entity. To comprehend this abstract concept is an arduous quest as she defies the limitations of form and attributes. Imagine, for a moment, seeing her in a magnificent golden robe sipping coffee. You might instinctively point and say, "Behold Sakshi!"

However, she is invisible to our sensory faculties — unseen by the eye, unheard by the ear, intangible to touch, and inconceivable by human perception.

Then, the question arises: how does one grasp the composition of such an entity? The Vedic scriptures suggest the 'neti-neti' technique, meaning neither this nor that. Instead of defining what the entity is, this method lists everything that it isn't. This technique of elimination helps fathom Sakshi since she is indescribable through words.

So we can start with a few things Sakshi is not. She does not keep a ledger of every creature's deeds to dispense judgment in the form of rewards or punishments. There are no bribes accepted, favors granted, or wrath inflicted by her. In her domain, there is no rigid definition of good or evil—only the impartial laws of nature and karma govern the course of all earthly events[5].

Another method to comprehend the abstract is through relatable symbols or metaphors that act as guides attempting to point toward the unknowable energy. Yet interpreting these symbolic representations too literally risks breeding misconstrued notions.

Consider this analogy to demonstrate how metaphors or pointers can be easily misunderstood: A guru points to the moon using a tree branch as a guide. Here, the moon represents the unknowable Sakshi, and the tree branch symbolizes the familiar concepts. He says, "Look at the moon on top of the tree branch." But if a seeker misunderstands the tree branch's role as a pointer and looks for the moon within the tree's branches, they might mistake an egg or fruit for the moon itself.

This, at least on some occasions, has resulted in breeding misinterpreted faiths over generations.

Given these complexities, perhaps it's best to just say that this eternal observer embodies the essence of everything that is and everything that will ever be—an omnipotent

---

[5] Bhagwad Gita Verse 5.14 - The (supreme eternal being) does not create people's ownership or actions, nor is it responsible for connecting fruits to action. Nature enacts everything in accordance with nature. See Appendix.

force transcending time and space. She represents the source of all creation and is the ultimate destination of all things.

The Vedas describe her as Purnam, denoting wholeness or absoluteness, while the Buddhists refer to her as Shunya, a term translating to zero or emptiness. Sakshi can be everything or no-thing (not nothing, it is not a thing). In a way, both everything and no-thing are concepts that exist in mutuality.

Echoes of this Vedic concept can be found in Stephen Hawking's contemplation of the origin of the universe from nothing. In his words, "According to one theory, the universe began with a Big Bang singularity. This theory is based on the idea that a law of nature, called 'zero-energy,' caused the universe to spring into existence from nothing.

This law says that the total energy in the universe is zero. The positive energy of matter and radiation is balanced by a negative energy of gravity."

Though Sakshi tirelessly transmits on every frequency, few sentient creatures can tune in with their cluttered minds - the incessant procession of thoughts and worries. The seeker must make the mental space, tune into the right frequency, and orient a pristine mind toward the broadcast to enable the reception.

We can all learn to be worthy seekers from the young boy Nachiket in Katha Upanishad[6]. The boy receives three boons from Yama, the lord of Death when he visits him in his palace. When Nachiket asks for enlightenment, Yama subjects him to tests employing a range of techniques to determine if he is worthy of being a "Seeker." He then warns Nachiket of the arduous journey ahead. One such example is verse 1.3.14, which urges one to "arise, awake," emphasizing that the path to self-knowledge is as difficult as walking on the sharp edge of a razor blade. The following verse describes why this is so challenging; it explains, "The ultimate reality is soundless, touchless, tasteless, odorless, without beginning or end, decayless, deathless, immutable, and unfathomably vast."

The path holds promise for even those who lack the complete qualifications that are prescribed by the scriptures.

---

[6] Katha Upanishad from Krishna Yajur Veda
1.3.14 uttiṣṭhata jāgrata, prāpya varānnibōdhata | kṣurasya dhārā niśitā duratyayā, durgaṁ pathastatkavayō vadanti | |
Arise. Awake.
Having approached the great (master), learn (the Self). The wise declare that the path (of Self-knowledge) is difficult to tread, (just as) the sharp edge of a razor is difficult to tread.

1.3.15   Aśabdamasparśamarūpamavyayaṁ,   tathārasaṁ
nityamagandhavacca yat | Anādyanantaṁ mahataḥ paraṁ dhruvaṁ,
nicāyya tanmṛtyumukhātpramucyatē | |
This is soundless, touchless, colorless, tasteless, smellless, beginningless, endless, decayless, deathless, changeless, and beyond infinity. Having clearly known that one is totally freed from the jaws of death.

31

We can still begin our journey - with a burning desire to uncover the truth, faith in ourselves, and a tranquil, focused mind.

We can all tune into the vibrations of Sakshi, which are thought to emanate from an eternal consciousness. Innumerable accounts exist of scholarly epiphanies arriving in dreams, creative inspirations in the shower, and mathematical proofs conceived on a quiet stroll - our mind tapping into transformative ideas through states of relaxation and presence. Though it's instinctive to attribute these experiences to the brain alone, science falls short, unable to identify the brain as the origin of these insights.

In 'Languages of the Brain,' Neuroscientist Karl Pribram proposes that the brain functions like a radio receiver. It captures signals from the senses and translates them into our perceived experiences. Extending this radio analogy, David Eagleman, in 'Incognito: The Secret Lives of the Brain,' points out that - extensively studying a radio won't reveal the nuances of its broadcast tower, a system distinct from the radio. Similarly, while studying the brain extensively can improve our insights into its functioning, it won't necessarily unravel the mysteries of consciousness.

Consciousness possesses unique features that set it apart from mere biological functions. These include our personal, subjective experiences like how the chocolate tastes or how a painting looks, the unity of diverse stimuli into a single perception, and our ability to reflect on our own thoughts. Essentially, it's the profound difference between simply processing information and having a personal, self-aware experience.

Let's return to that distant realm or perhaps stay within the confines of our minds to watch today's broadcast. It centers around the elusive pursuit of happiness, a timeless quest that has entangled humanity throughout the ages.

With a serene aura, Sakshi commences her message by first introducing herself: "I am the past, present, and future, plus everything else that exists beyond the three time periods through multi-verses in multiple dimensions. I am not the universe. The universe is a manifestation of me, but it is only an illusion. I am the unchanging reality."[7]

Maya walks in as Sakshi continues broadcasting. Her presence commands fascination - cinnamon eyes gleaming playfully paired with her auburn curls and olive complexion.

---

[7]This introduction of Sakshi is inspired by the first Mantra of Mandukya Upanishad, the shortest and most potent. In the epic Ramayana, when Hanuman asked Lord Ram how to attain liberation, Ram directed him to this Upanishad. The first Mantra states:
hariḥ om | om ityetad akṣaram idaṃ sarvaṃ tasy upavyākhyānaṃ bhūtaṃ bhavad bhaviṣyad iti sarvam oṅkāra eva | yacc ānyat trikālātītaṃ tad api oṅkāra eva
Om is the symbol of Brahma. It represents everything in the universe in the past, present, and future and everything else that exists beyond the three-time periods.

She is draped in a jewel-toned Persian turquoise tunic glittering with silver paisley brocade.

Maya is the embodiment of reality's grand illusion we know as the universe. Her charisma fills the space as she delights in her role of bridging Sakshi's vast wisdom with the comprehension of ordinary humans.

Understanding the intricacies of illusion better than anyone else, she asks with a knowing smile, "But how are the creatures in the cosmos supposed to know that their world is an illusion?"

Maya's question prompts Sakshi to simplify her message. Sakshi explains, "Think of how colors, shapes, depth of spaces, and everything else in the world around you only exist because you are conscious of it. The color you see arises from an object reflecting certain wavelengths of light. These wavelengths are picked up by the photoreceptors in your retina and translated into electrical signals for your brain. Essentially, the object exists only in your perception. In a way, all things you sense — what you see, hear, smell, touch, or feel — exist only in your mind. Without your awareness, your world ceases to exist."

Chapter 3: The Happiness Mirage

Having witnessed countless cycles of the universe's creation and destruction, Maya has a timeless perspective of all its underpinnings. Yet, the illusion's multifaceted beauty consistently captivates her. "What's the theme of today's session?" she inquires, pouring the hot, fragrant brew into her cup.

Sakshi: "Happiness - Everyone's goal in life comes down to being happy. So let's talk about happiness."

Maya: "What truly defines happiness? A smile, a laugh, a certain mood?"

Sakshi: "You can say it's a state of mind. For example, if it rains, you can either be bothered with the water all over your clothes and shoes or feel the joy of being alive and enjoy the sensations."

Intrigued, Maya counters, "If it is a matter of choice, then why are humans not always happy."

Anticipating the question, Sakshi smiles. "Ahh...yes," she says, "it is because of the misunderstanding of where happiness is sourced from. You see, humans believe that happiness comes solely from the physical world around them. They determine desirability based on pleasurable sensations, avoiding unpleasant ones like pain or discomforting tastes, sights, or smells. They work tirelessly to build a particular lifestyle that gives them easy access to objects of physical gratification and are quick to avoid things that displease their senses. It could be…"

Maya, sensing potential confusion in the audience, speaks up. "Just to clarify, we are currently focused on physical experiences because they are often the simplest to grasp. While some of what's discussed can be related to intellectual and emotional experiences, we will delve deeper into those areas later."

Sakshi nods appreciatively, "Yes. Thank you, Maya, for that clarification." She continues, "Humans strive to fulfill their desires, and, at some point, they may achieve them. Getting what they want makes them very happy. However, the joy is relatively short-lived.

Unfortunately, after their wishes are granted, the pleasure experienced at any moment is inversely proportional to the length of time after acquisition. For example, say you wanted that dream house, an exotic vacation, a designer piece of clothing, or recognition at work. You were sure back then that getting the object of your desire would make you happy. So you struggled, did what you had to, and made your aspirations come true. That one moment when the desire is fulfilled feels incredibly rewarding! Yet, ask yourself, how long did that euphoria truly last?"

Sakhi continues her transmission for the humans tuning in. "Invariably, the thrill fades as desires are quenched. You end up needing more of it or something bigger, better, shinier to sustain the happiness."

As the resonance of Sakshi's words permeates the space, Maya delves deeper with a key question necessary to illuminate core human strivings. Noticing Sakshi's deep meditative state, she silently floats up her query.

"How does one find that permanent, unchanging state of happiness?"

Sakshi's voice resonates with tranquility as she answers, "The world around you is constantly changing, and you have no control over when, how, and what changes will come. If your happiness depends on worldly things, it will inevitably fluctuate with the changing tides. The logical path to persistent well-being lies in unhooking your state of happiness from the external world."

Maya is visibly excited in anticipation of Sakshi's answer as she asks, "But how can you simply unhook from the world?"

Sakshi responds, "You do that by seeing through its illusion." Then, realizing Maya's enthusiasm, she encourages her, "Since none know illusion better than anyone else, please unveil this truth."

Eager to unravel the mystery, Maya dives right in, 'The planet created for you is not just a realm of vivid colors and delightful sounds, but a mosaic of experiences you perceive through your sensory inputs. However, your senses allow you to perceive only a fraction of the boundless beauty surrounding you. Beyond your direct experience lies an unseen realm of wonder – a symphony of sensations that elude your grasp due to the limitations of your physical form.

While you can feel the tantalizing warmth of the sun's rays on a chilly morning through your skin and see the dance of shimmering auroras of northern lights, you cannot even imagine what it would be like to experience the countless vibrations and energies from the invisible heat to the ultrasonic sounds, all forming an exquisite symphony of existence.

Every living being[8], whether it roams the land, navigates the sea, or soars through the sky, perceives the world uniquely through its set of senses. The evidence of this diversity is everywhere. For instance, bats use ultrasonic sounds to find their way through pitch-dark nights, while sharks trace their underwater routes using electric fields.

Sea turtles, driven by an innate compass, embark on epic journeys across vast oceans, following the pull of the Earth's

---

[8] This section is inspired by the works of science writer Ed Young.

magnetic field. Bees, with their microscopic eyes, are wired to spot ultraviolet lights. The deep waters echo with the low-frequency songs of whales relaying news of food sources or potential dangers over great distances.

Elephants, with their earthen wisdom, tune into the rhythmic vibrations of the planet to map out their route over long distances, which is remembered through generations. None of these signals can be sensed by a human body. The diversity of the raw material used to build the world ensures that each creature has its own realm that is hidden from all others.

With such finite senses as a human, it becomes essential to question whether your perspective encompasses the full breadth of what is. Can you genuinely claim to hold a complete understanding of existence when you cannot experience most things right around you?

Freeing reliance on the senses will allow you to humbly recognize the vastness of the unseen. By doing so, you can see through the mirage. Your physical body enables you to taste flavors, smell fragrances, see colors and shapes, hear melodies, and feel textures. However, the magic you perceive is woven within the mind, which assigns meanings to the sensory inputs received in the brain. It is the mind that conjures up the world from the limited inputs available."

"The world exists within you - was so beautifully explained," says Sakshi, nudging Maya to reveal the climax.

"Right," Maya continues, taking Sakshi's cue, "but you see, the function of the mind goes beyond the mere act of conjuring the illusion. As the primary interpreter of these sensations, the mind filters the raw signals through the lens of past experiences, cultural influences, and personal biases. It fabricates intricate stories, constructing narratives about the external world and internal feelings. This process is where desires and anguish are born.

Desires arise when the mind clings to pleasurable sensations and craves their repetition or amplification. Conversely, anxiety emerges when the mind resists or seeks to avoid unpleasant feelings. Thus, the mind becomes the source of pleasure and suffering.

The human mind has an uncanny ability to create stories, deeply influencing our perception of the world and our place within it. Consider something as rudimentary as a piece of paper – a dollar bill. It has no utility and, by itself, cannot offer sustenance, warmth, or shelter. However, humans can ascribe symbolic value to the paper, so it represents far more than its physical form; it represents a complex narrative of economic systems, societal agreements, and shared beliefs." Maya elaborates.

Building on Maya's thoughts, Sakshi adds, "While the human mind's capacity for storytelling can lead to extraordinary feats and cooperation on a grand scale, it has equal potential to inflict suffering. The inclinations and aversions you experience are a direct result of the stories you choose to believe in."

In my view, the next vital step becomes recognizing these stories for what they are - fleeting illusions woven by the mind.

This extraordinary ability to generate and believe in fiction can be both a gift and a curse. We all know this at some level. But for those still entangled in samsara's complexities, how do we navigate this web?

Buddha's approach to battling the suffering of the world was to give up all worldly attachments completely. However, not everyone can give up their family and responsibilities in search of lasting peace.

The Gita, in contrast, presents a more accessible approach. It teaches the seeker to be dispassionate while remaining fully functional in the world. Chapter 2, verse 70[9],

---

[9] Bhagwad Gita Verse 2.70 - The person who can absorb all the desires, like the ocean, absorbs all the water (from the rivers) pouring into it while being steady and undisturbed is the one who attains peace. And not the one who follows the dictates of the desires or passion. See appendix.

summarizes the core concept with an inspiring metaphor of the ocean. Even as raging currents from mighty rivers surge into it during monsoon, the ocean remains unaffected. In the ocean's tranquility, churning waves pose no turmoil, their frenzy incapable of affecting its silent depths. Through this unperturbed poise, stormy waves are transformed into clouds and rain that will nourish lands.

Similarly, the wise remain unmoved by the massive force of desirable and undesirable events all around them. While they stay inwardly unshakable, they act in the world to subtly steer turmoil's energies towards the highest good.

It is this paradoxical attribute of the illusion that makes it a captivating ride. Maya wants every embodied being to enjoy this grand evanescent illusion while seeing through it when needed. It is like if you watch a movie, you want to be immersed in it. But not affected by it because it is only a movie.

Switching from the metaphysical to the mundane, Maya illustrates her point further. "For example, consider your desire for a molten chocolate cake," Maya continues. "if the narrative is that you lack self-control and cannot resist, this belief can be detrimental to other aspects of life. But realizing it simply triggers reward centers makes the draw more understandable.

Now, you become an intrigued and dispassionate observer of your body and mind's reaction to the cake. Suddenly, the cake no longer has the same hold on you.

You do not have to indulge in it because, through your observations, you already know that the pleasure is transitory and inconsequential. You also do not need to shun it completely if eating the cake gives joy to the person celebrating their birthday.

In short, you are really unattached to the pleasure - not really chasing it and not trying to escape from it either."

Sakshi meets Maya's gaze as she adds, "You can extend this approach to anything that you find attractive or repulsive. By analyzing your desires and aversions, you can become detached and liberated. As you shift into observation, beware of the mind trying to pull you back into its narratives."

Maya nods in agreement and then continues, "How remarkably the mind wields its power of perception by weaving meaningful stories from the threads of our sensory experiences.

By training this director of our inner movie to observe all the sensations without judgment, we can see through the deception of what parades itself as reality. As dispassionate observers, simply witnessing the rush of imagery without labeling villains or victims, heroes or horrors, we can navigate the duality of pleasure and pain. The body and physical senses can be the chariot of a discerning mind."

After pausing to allow the vibrations of her message to settle, Maya gently steers the conversation in a new direction. "Now, moving on to the next source of joy," she says, "What about the happiness you experience from being fully engaged in an activity? That seems like a pretty stable source of happiness. Time almost stops; the stream of thoughts from the past or worries of the future disappear. There is complete peace."

Sakshi: "Yes, this is the state of "flow."[10] It works well as long as you can find it. The activity must be moderately demanding to fully occupy the intellect. This leaves no space for any other thoughts except for reflective self-awareness. If the task becomes too difficult, there is a chance you get frustrated. If the task is too simple, the mind will have the additional bandwidth to dwell on the past or worry about the future. The activity must achieve the Goldilocks' level of perfection.

The intense concentration period can give a sense of control in an otherwise unpredictable world. However, you may not always be able to find that perfect flow in all the things you

---

[10] The Hungarian psychologist Mihaly Csikszentmihalyi pioneered the research on the "flow" state. When studying artists and creative types, Mihaly observed that the act of creating seemed more important than the finished work itself.

will need to do in your role. So, any happiness depending on anything worldly cannot offer stability, and you know why!"

"Yes, it is because the world is ever-changing!" responds Maya, sounding pleased that they have come full circle on two primary sources of joy - physical and intellectual.

After a moment of reflection, allowing the recipients to absorb the truth, Maya prepares to move on to the third source of joy: emotional Contemplating the origin of emotional well-being, she asks, "Let us delve now into emotional wells of happiness - the elation arising from praises of great achievements, breakthroughs, discoveries, compositions or paintings. Shouldn't the joy from accomplishments endure?"

As Sakshi and Maya deliberate, an energy familiar to both of them begins to ripple through the space, heralding the arrival of a kindred spirit. Suddenly, a triumphant voice interjects, "Well, all monumental feats, or lack of them, are entirely out of human control. I am to be credited for every achievement and deficit." The familiar voice of their old friend Prakruti fills the space.

"Sorry I am late," says Prakruti, her long ebony hair swirling around her like a cascading waterfall, contrasting her luminescent brown skin. She glides gracefully toward her friends, her moss green satin gown clings lightly as if it were

45

a part of her form. As the ageless **laws of nature** manifested, she governs the functioning of existence.

The trio bursts into a loud roar of laughter at Prakruti's unabashed assertion of claiming all credit. As the broadcast nears its end, it's time to start a lighthearted game of cards.

Sakshi's airy voice fills existence as she concludes the broadcast with a sprinkle of playfulness. "Remember, life's greatest game is in discovering your true self or perhaps in finding me. It's a quest filled with surprises and adventures. Enjoy the ride of being a human and watch out for the deceptions of your exquisite worlds," she says, sounding more like a theme park guide than a philosopher.

With a hint of what's to come, she teases her next episode, promising insights on happiness from achievements, and exploring nature with Prakruti and Maya.

Chapter 4: Making the Elephant Dance

Qayum wakes up with a jolt. The remnants of her dream still linger at the edge of her mind as she glances at the clock, noticing it's just a few minutes before her alarm will sound. It feels as though she had been tumbling through the vastness of space, only to abruptly land back in her bed, wide awake.

She tries to recall the dream that seemed so enchanting, a place of beauty with a rushing river, majestic banyan trees, and the warmth of friends' laughter. Yet, the details slip away like grains of sand escaping a clenched fist.

Taking a deep breath, she closes her eyes and tries to return to her serene dream. "That's not how it works!" an inner voice reminds.

Just then the alarm summons her to take on the day.

Reluctantly, she rises and prepares for her morning run. Outside, a gentle breeze welcomes her, and she finds a narrow trail tucked among the redwoods surrounding her cottage. Running has always been her refuge, grounding her in the present moment. Though not an athlete, she maintains a slow, steady jog each morning, savoring the sense of liberation it brings. As she settles into the familiar tempo of her run, the mind whips a new stream of thoughts, blending old memories and fresh insights.

During the final decade of her all-consuming career, trying to scale the ranks of the tech elite, Qayum willingly shouldered ever-mounting responsibilities, embracing the mantra that Silicon Valley stalwarts were forged in fires of non-stop perfection.

Over time, though, as the technical challenges failed to sufficiently stimulate her ambitious mind, Qayum found herself losing steam. As her career transitioned onto an administrative track, Qayum's drive curdled to disillusionment. Once clearly mapped, highways towards the upper echelons later lead instead to the mazelike corridors of middle management.

The weight of perceived setbacks now extended beyond her workday, constantly challenging her very sense of self. Endless hours were spent lost in introspection. Turning to philosophical texts she desperately hunted for that elusive sense of purpose she recalled once knowing in her youth's simple devotion.

The relentless drive and pace exacted its toll, inexorably sliding her down the slippery slope toward utter exhaustion.

Sleep became a precious commodity, often sacrificed for the demands of product launches, customer escalations, and team management issues. And when sleep eventually did claim her, nightmares would steal her peace.

These dreams had a pattern: faceless entities or figures from her past and present would chase her, their intentions obscure. In her sleep, she ran through dreamscapes of forests and cities, some vividly real while others were like a flat canvas drawn by an artist's hand. But always, the pursuer was close behind. She would wake up frightened and try to rewrite the endings of these troubling night terrors punctuated by the jarring sound of the alarm.

After leaving the tech industry, the nightmares faded away. Yet, last night's dream stood out. It felt authentic and unlike the dandelion-fluff of most dreams. The vision was like a buried memory resurfacing from the depths of her being and offering an answer to her question on the volatility of happiness.

The answer seems so obvious now.

Her thoughts flow, "Life is like an ever-shifting kaleidoscope. Each twist displays a stunning pattern of colors and shapes, distinct and volatile in its beauty. Our mind then assigns meanings to these patterns, forming desires and aversions.

Change remains the one true constant. Even when we capture that one perfect twist where everything in our world is as we would want it to be, in the next moment, the world invariably shifts. Whether it's unexpected bills, a loved one's illness, a setback at work, a plan thwarted, or a close friend moving away, even a single shift disrupts our fragile state of bliss.

Thus, true, enduring happiness requires that we detach our inner well-being from the capriciousness of the external world. We need to rewrite the stories that dictate our likes and dislikes."

"Ha! It is easier said than done," Qayum murmurs to her insightful thought and picks up her pace, navigating the winding trail with ease.

She wonders, "We envision change readily yet struggle to actualize it. Why is it so hard to make a change even when we are convinced of the value it adds to our lives?"

Recalling some of the books she has read in the past, her mind synthesizes, "This mystery is deeply rooted in the evolutionary development of the brain. Originating millions of years ago, the **amygdala** stands as the oldest part of our brain, governing motor functions and rapidly processing sensory inputs to trigger instinctive responses to threats. For our ancestors, this swift and automatic response was necessary for survival. The amygdala, basically, is the brain's primary center, orchestrating our most primal fears and emotions.

While the ancient amygdala excels at snappy emotional judgments, a more recent **pre-frontal cortex** serves as the epicenter for advanced faculties like logical reasoning, strategic planning, and abstract computations. It is a relatively recent addition and testament to our species' cognitive evolution. However, such sophistication comes at a price. Engaging the pre-frontal cortex demands more metabolic energy compared to the amygdala's reflexive, energy-efficient operations."

The narratives and perceptions that define our likes and dislikes, joys and sorrows, are deeply ingrained within the amygdala. This hardwiring, honed over millennia, makes it formidable to rewrite or challenge these narratives. Renowned psychologist Daniel Kahneman delves into this interplay with his dichotomy of System 1 (instinctual) and System 2 (deliberate) thinking in his book 'Thinking, Fast and Slow.'

In a parallel analogy, Jonathan Haidt invokes the imagery of the elephant and its rider. The elephant symbolizes the powerful yet untamed amygdala, which often forges ahead, driven by primal impulses. The rider, representing the pre-frontal cortex, possesses the foresight and strategic wisdom to navigate the journey. However, even this enlightened rider must grapple with the elephant's sheer might. Asserting control and teaching the elephant new ways necessitates an odyssey of disciplined, consistent effort, often spanning years, if not a lifetime.

Qayum lives this tension between the amygdala and cortex every morning as her impulses resist routine discipline. An

51

elephant swayed by instinct and the mahout guiding with wisdom gained over time is the ongoing dance between two disparate partners.

Today, the mahout managed to coax the elephant out of bed and into the forest for a jog. She steadies her pace and intentionally deepens her breaths. The air is nippy, infused with scents of pine and refreshing eucalyptus. The forest drapes in tranquil silence, the rhythmic crunch of dry pine needles and redwood bark under her feet occasionally interrupted by the chirrups of birds.

With each step, Qayum's body relaxes further, attuned to the rhythm of her motion. Eventually, she reaches a clearing surrounded by towering trees that seem to touch the sky, and in the distance, she can see the gleaming, calm ocean. Settling on a rock, she closes her eyes and focuses on her breath.

Over the past few years, Qayum had devoted herself to gaining control over her physical senses. Her ambitions were to go beyond being a mahout; she wanted to make her elephant dance in harmony with the melodies of life. At the beginning of her journey, her body resisted every attempt to shape its behavior. It would protest, demanding more sleep even after a restful night or feign fatigue to avoid exercise, later lying awake in the night, engrossed in replays of past events or potential futures. Succumbing to these demands only strengthened her body's defiance.

Eventually, **three** complementary tools emerged: **first**, leverage automation through habits; second, detach from the mind's strong opinions; and third, maintain equanimity by tearing the false boundaries between pleasurable and unpleasant.

A significant breakthrough arrived when Qayum chanced upon an intriguing research paper probing into the science of habit formations. The study uncovered that each decision, whether instinctual or calculated, directly influences the habits we develop.

For instance, when feeling tired in the morning, the instinctual thought may be to hit snooze and sleep in. However, the conscious decision to wake up and start the day has the potential to form the habit of rising early. Similarly, hitting the snooze button will allow that to become a habit. She marveled - who would have guessed that mundane acts like choosing between hitting snooze or rising could leave physical traces, subtly redirecting future decisions etched in neuronal pathways.

Within each individual, there exists a constant interplay of competing thoughts, all vying for dominance in their actions and choices. Each decision, primal or deliberate, hardens that particular aspect of the personality. Over time, the competing thoughts that did not get chosen lose strength and grow softer or die out. This is the process of formation of both helpful and detrimental habits.

This insight helped to deal with the mind's auto-generated requests like "Let's skip this only today. We can start on it tomorrow. Tomorrow will be a much better day to start because.." To this very compelling offer, Qayum's mahout would say, "Let's just focus on today and not worry about what happens tomorrow. There might not be a tomorrow. We will just do it today. We will start slow. Let's do it only today!" She hoped that with time, a habit would form and the negotiations could be skipped.

The process, however, is slow, like the river etching canyons through the mountains. Repetition and consistency are needed, and that is what makes the process so hard.

The analogy of the elephant and its mahout has limitations. In many ways, it fails to fully capture the complex dynamics at play. The amygdala, unlike the elephant, responds very quickly and takes no effort. In contrast, the pre-frontal cortex operates slowly and burns significant calories like a strenuous workout.

When Qayum grew tired, hungry, or irritable, the elephant did as it pleased, and the mahout was nowhere to be found. She also realized that the rider had limited energy, depleting much like a battery pack that required time and rest to recharge. If she exerted her willpower to do things her psyche resisted, she found herself with no drive left for the next negotiation. The quantity of this precious energy expended depended on how strongly her primal instincts were set against the actions that her thinking mind deemed essential.

To address the limitations of willpower, the **second** technique comes into play, aiming to temper the intensity of joy or distress associated with any object or experience. The idea was that if the elephant was not feeling so intense in its desire or aversion, it might hear the feeble calls of the mahout, even when the mahout had less willpower left to reason with the elephant.

In his book "Conquest of Mind," Eknath Easwaran challenges the reader to playfully toss up their preferences and freely juggle them, converting likes to dislikes and vice-versa. This game of non-attachment, if you can have fun doing it, can loosen the grip of cravings for certain foods, activities, or comforts while also weakening the power of aversions, making them easier to overcome when necessary.

For instance, one can willingly agree to visit a restaurant they dislike if their partner enjoys it, perform dull household chores without complaint, or watch a movie a friend wants to see, even if it fails to pique their own interest.

Easwaran argues we often mistakenly equate our likes with rational choices and dislikes with justified avoidance. In truth, we are driven by transient desires and instincts that overpower reason. As Easwaran eloquently states, "We tell ourselves, 'I like this, so I do it. I don't like that, so I do not bother with it.' What we really mean is, 'I'm in a car that turns on its own accord. I can't help going after things I like, and I can't help avoiding things I dislike.'"

There is a similar and perhaps more famous Chariot analogy from Katha Upanishad (Mantras 1.3.3-11). Here, the true self is metaphorically the rider or the lord of the chariot. The body serves as the chariot propelled by the horses, representing the five senses. The intellect, symbolized by the charioteer, holds the reins, which equate to the mind.

For most beings, neither the rider nor the charioteer seems to be in control of the reins. Instead, our lives are steered by the untrained senses, leading us wherever they please.

Her ingrained likes and dislikes fueled the amygdala's instinctive reactions, making it harder for the prefrontal cortex to assert conscious control. When such impulses were strong, enormous willpower was required to override them.

Furthermore, she noticed that her presumed preferences were not actually deliberate but rather subconscious conditioning through associations that sparked aversion or pleasure. Initially, it was hard for her to distinguish between the involuntary preferences molded by evolution, genetics, and upbringing and the intentional choices she made for their perceived benefits.

Since the distinction between likes and dislikes mostly lives in our psyche, she employed the **third** technique from her toolkit - equalizing opposing circumstances.

When overloaded by attraction or aversion to the physical world, she would imagine the opposite scenario and observe her body's reaction. The practice enabled her to find equanimity when tested by the most enticing or repulsive stimuli.

Right now, exhilarated by the serenity of the woods, she transports her mind to a chaotic slum of Mumbai, close to her childhood home, where the stench of rotting garbage and fecal matter prevailed. She witnesses her senses recoil in disgust. Questioning herself, she wonders if she could find the same calmness in that slum.

After some struggle, she manages to envision the peace she feels now, even with the city's cacophony and grime around her. While she does not yet possess the necessary expertise or immediate control over her mind and body to enact it, in her imagination, she weaves this serenity seamlessly. The exercise has planted the seeds for her future growth.

Qayum learned this particular practice of envisioning opposites from the Stoic philosophers. The Stoics perceived all the dualities in the world – such as light and darkness, fortune and misfortune, happiness and sorrow – as two sides of the same coin that balance each other out.

For example, they recognized that light requires darkness to exist and vice versa; you cannot have one without the other. Similarly, favorable circumstances inevitably give rise to adversity as part of the natural cycle of change.

The Stoics saw these opposites as coexisting in harmony, each containing the seed of the other. Therefore, they cautioned against having extreme emotional reactions to any single situation, whether positive or negative. In their view, every circumstance merely signaled the inevitable emergence of its opposite coming next.

To practice control over despair, many Stoics would vividly visualize the loss of valued possessions, honor, or even health. By imagining the worst-case scenarios, they were equipped to overcome any adversity with equanimity.

On the flip side, to moderate their desire and ambitions, Stoics would envision having whatever they currently lacked - wealth, status, material comforts. By picturing themselves as already content and fulfilled, they aimed to curb excessive desires.

Initially, this Stoic practice seemed absurd to Qayum. During pleasant moments, she questioned why she should spoil it by imagining unpleasant scenarios. It felt unnecessary when life readily supplied enough challenges and torment anyway.

However, she soon discovered the power of this technique after sustained practice. Visualizing opposites built her mental resilience. It enabled her to easily envision maintaining inner tranquility and poise, even through intense adversity.

As a result, neither the desirable nor the unfavorable in the physical world held sway over her happiness as intensely as before. This dance toward self-mastery stretched onward, discipline and perseverance plotted against temptation and surrender, with missteps sometimes outnumbering progress. Even so, in a world of constant change, Qayum had found a measure of control to navigate life's unpredictable tides.

Detaching from the world to find persistent peace goes beyond worldly temptations and shaping personal preferences. While Qayum has made strides in remaining unfazed by the allure of the physical world, she recognizes that true detachment demands more. It means being unaffected by the dualities of success and failures, honor and dishonor.

The final veils of attachment still awaited unraveling to reveal the outdated roles and self-limiting stories still binding her.

Yet, in this moment, there is tranquility. She centers herself with a deep inhalation, filling her lungs with eucalyptus-laden fresh air. Then begins the ancient chant:

Oṃ Sarveṣāṃ svastir bhavatu |
Sarveṣāṃ śāntir bhavatu |
Sarveṣāṃ pūrṇam bhavatu |
Sarveṣāṃ maṅgalam bhavatu |
Oṃ śāntiḥ śāntiḥ śāntiḥ hii | |
Let there be good health and well-being for all beings.

Let there be peace for all beings.
Let there be abundance for all beings.
Let there be favorable outcomes for all beings.
Let there be peace, peace, peace.

Although Qayum turned agnostic in her adult life, chanting these ancient Sanskrit verses held deeper meaning for her - not tied to any dogmas, but rather as selfless moments sending positive vibrations out into the ether. The rhythmic demands and precise enunciation of Sanskrit challenged her mind to remain focused on the words and her breath as she chanted.

However, once a mantra became too familiar, its syllables flowing automatically, her mind could recite and often wander simultaneously. When this happened, she knew it was time to switch to another mantra with fresh patterns still meaningful to contemplate.

The mantra she had often repeated during her daily meditation ritual some time ago floated back to her now, the resonant words and rhythms still etched into her memory. She reaches back to its stirring syllables:

Oṃ Sarve bhavantu sukhinaḥ |
Sarve santu nirāmayāḥ |
Sarve bhadrāni paśyantu |
mā kaścid dukḥ bhāgbhavet |
Oṃ śāntiḥ śāntiḥ śāntiḥ hii | |

Let all beings be at peace.
Let all beings be free from illness.
Let all beings see good fortune.
Let no one suffer.
Let there be peace, peace, peace.

Part 2: The Detached

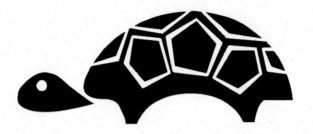

Like the tortoise draws its limbs into its shell, the people seeking self-realization withdraw from the physical senses. They are everywhere without attachment, receiving the positive without rejoicing and the negative without avoiding. They are on the right path.[11]

---

[11] Rephrased Bhagwad Gita Verses 2.57 and 2.58. See appendix.

Chapter 5: Stuck in the Past

Within just a few minutes, Qayum's mind drifts back to thinking of detachment from worldly ups and downs. A gentle ocean breeze brushes against her skin as the mind travels to memories of Umati, the ruthless engineering leader from her past corporate life. The beauty and serenity of the woods overlooking the deep blue ocean fade as events from the past begin to resurface.

Umati had cunningly assembled a team of influential individuals, employing tactics of bullying, bribing, or obliterating others to enforce unending loyalty to her. She ceaselessly pursued superiority for her engineering projects, and whenever another team presented a better project, she launched relentless attacks to hinder or eliminate their projects. The pervasive fear of her loomed large and was a constant reminder that anyone who would cross her would lose their job.

When Qayum first joined the company, many friendly team members warned her about Umati, but she laughed off their cautionary tales. It all sounded too Machiavellian to be true. Besides, this was a company Qayum had dreamed of working at, boasting some of the most brilliant minds in the industry.

In her early days, Qayum found it hard to believe Umati's rumored brutality could exist there. But soon, her visible project caught Umati's eye. Qayum presented the project plan to a large audience at the all-hands meeting, and naturally, Umati wanted to meet her immediately after.

Their first encounter unsettled Qayum. Umati made peculiar remarks about her own manager, Bimal, lips twisting wryly, "You can say we are like, 'Buy one, get one half off!' Haha."

Umati insisted Qayum "get aligned" with them but remained purposefully ambiguous. Qayum's project was already funded, so what did alignment mean? Anxiety stirred as Umati clarified that Qayum wasn't using her team's tool, though it clearly didn't suit Qayum's customer needs.

Visibly annoyed, Umati persisted, and while a disoriented Qayum pondered her response, Umati steered the conversation toward critiquing Qayum's senior leadership, "I hear he completely botched the recent strategy session."

Qayum choked back tears as she managed to say that her leadership was great. She wanted to retort, "How dare you?" but her voice failed her, and courage eluded her.

Umati questioned with a frown, "Great! you say?" Her words were laced with disgust. "Well, I've heard that strategy misses the mark entirely. It is stale and fluff with no substance...," she said sharply before turning her attention to her laptop and announcing that she was needed elsewhere. The damage was dealt.

Qayum was relieved to get out of the meeting. She did not want to believe what had just happened. She wondered if her reaction to the situation was excessive. Maybe Umati did not mean anything bad. Perhaps it was just a difference in style. Qayum did not care much about Bimal because, at that time, he was not in her "food chain" and had no impact on her projects. Umati could create roadblocks. Qayum wondered if those stories she had heard about Umati were true.

Over the next few months, Qayum heard rumors, all somehow traced back to Umati. The tall tales portrayed Qayum as someone who was bad at communicating with customers, taking credit for others' work, and lacking knowledge in her field.

Initially, Qayum laughed them off, dismissing them as obviously untrue. But the whispers and gossip soon began to wield a predictable influence on her projects.

Qayum believed meeting face-to-face could resolve their differences. But Umati constantly rescheduled. Even joining her "women's support group" proved futile.

So, Qayum got busy working on several other projects. Everyone around her admired her ability to propose solutions to elusive technical problems. She became the go-to person when a new business problem needed to be solved or there was a fire to put out. Her team loved her, her boss frequently appreciated and rewarded her, and her peers were very protective of her. Most days, Qayum even forgot that Umati existed. She had closed that chapter in her mind.

Yet, fate had a different plan. An HR case was filed against Umati, handled by George, Bimal's superior, who sought insights into her behavior.

One morning, Qayum sat down with George, hesitant to speak out unless he assured her of protection from Umati and Bimal. Reassured by his confirmation of multiple complaints, she decided to share everything.

George acknowledged her feedback aligned with others and expressed intent to take immediate action with HR. Qayum thanked him, holding on to hope that justice was about to be served.

When Qayum explained to George about Bimal's role in encouraging Umati's behavior, he confirmed that it was precisely for this reason that he was personally handling the case.

So, it made no sense when George placed Qayum and her team under Bimal's authority in the recent reorganization. The murmurs in the hallways all echoed with confusion, "So strange!" Then, even more peculiar events started to unfold.

Qayum was on the promotion committee, holding the critical task of determining the promotion of three women and three men. The guidelines were explicit. The managers of the nominees were present solely to address any queries. Additionally, each nominee had another senior colleague from their team to sponsor them and make a case for their promotion.

However, the situation became challenging when Bimal, now Qayum's superior, entered the picture. Ideally, Bimal should not have attended the meeting, and even if he did, he was expected to remain neutral and refrain from influencing the committee's decision. These regulations were essential to ensure the committee's autonomy in making its recommendations. Ultimately, it would be the VP who could choose to override the committee's suggestions. The entire process was meticulously documented for HR's records.

At the promotion committee session, Bimal couldn't resist providing ongoing commentary. He made remarks about a woman who had delivered a project surpassing expectations for her grade level, stating, "It is important to put people from the right grade on the job." On another occasion, when everyone else had acknowledged another woman's outstanding performance, Bimal peculiarly declared, "I will not say anything because I have worked with her before."

Each time Bimal made his cryptic comments, Nandan, who was directing the committee meeting, appeared to be influenced, swiftly moving the candidates to the lower end of the list or even marking them as ineligible for promotion.

67

Despite protests from other members, Nandan waved them off, insisting, "We need to move on for now; we can revisit this at the end."

Then it was Anish's turn—a fairly inexperienced individual who lacked initiative, only doing what he was asked to do. However, Bimal confidently declared, "Anish's promotion is a no-brainer. Let's move on to the next person." When someone objected, highlighting the importance of initiative at the next grade level, Bimal brazenly credited Anish with efforts he was not involved in. Who could challenge Bimal's claim or provide evidence of his deception?

Regrettably, all three highly capable women were made ineligible, while the three men were put up for promotion.

These remarkable women were currently at lower grades than their male counterparts, yet they had consistently outperformed expectations. Determined to put up resistance against this grave injustice, Qayum felt her heart racing as she gathered all her courage.

Nandan made the final call for objections, attempting to conclude the meeting. Just then, the committee's "diversity police" raised his hand.

The 'diversity police' was an informal title for a member who ensured that the promotion process was free from biases and that the committee upheld the principles of diversity and inclusion. His role was to act as a watchdog, making sure that everyone got a fair chance, regardless of their gender, race, or any other factor.

The room was thick with suspense, everyone eager to hear his intervention. Qayum was filled with hope and prepared to offer her own support. In an unexpected anticlimax, the man holding the diversity police role instead said, "I want to express my gratitude to Bimal for gracing us with his presence and staying neutral throughout the discussion. He is truly a great leader."

Qayum's jaw dropped in disbelief, her resistance crumbling like a fragile fortress as the reality of the situation sunk in. She felt a piercing ache in her chest but managed to hide her emotions. Nandan was visibly relieved and chimed in with more praise for Bimal.

The atmosphere in the room became tense and uncomfortable, clearly displaying the divide between the two camps of people. On one side were those who felt unwilling and helpless participants of the charade, silently understanding the underlying issues but feeling powerless or scared to say anything.

On the other side were those who seemed content to play their part, either oblivious or indifferent to the unfairness of the proceedings.

Qayum found the entire episode preposterous. Would anyone else believe it? With Umati as the only woman promoted in Bimal's org, the situation seemed even more glaring.

"Wait! What about the HR case?" Qayum asked Nandan, still grappling with the injustice. "What did you think was going to happen? And do you remember the manager who argued with Bimal at the promotion committee for the woman on his team?" he asked, seeking her understanding. Qayum nodded, curious about the manager's fate. "Well, he is in a lot of trouble," sighed Nandan, hoping Qayum would finally understand the repercussions that awaited those who dared to challenge the status quo.

In the aftermath of this disheartening experience, a part of Qayum turned cold and lifeless. She resolutely focused on her work, her team, and her customers, finding solace and purpose in those realms while keeping her anger and frustration buried deep within.

The rousing caress of a passing redwood breeze gently nudges Qayum's awareness and draws her back into the present. Though the process of reliving the old memory lasted only a few minutes, the weight and intensity drags her down. It fills the present moment with heaviness and perplexes her.

In the midst of a serene meditation session, why would she think of the past? why does this memory cling to her like a sticky, stubborn residue, refusing to let go? She tries to shake it off to escape its suffocating grip.

The answer to Qayum's questions lies in the all-powerful amygdala's evolutionary advantage of responding to threats with intensity. Not only does it possess the quickest access to our motor functions, but it also wields control over the narratives of our memories.

In particular, we tend to focus on the negative as it has an evolutionary advantage. It helped our ancestors avoid danger and be more responsive.

The problem with the **negative cognitive bias** is that we often remember the one bad event over the many, many good things that occurred during the same period.

Furthermore, Qayum's perception is unavoidably flawed. The stage for the drama to unfold was already set up when the pre-warnings from her colleagues primed her view of Umati as threatening before they even met. With this initial bias set, all interactions fed that threatening narrative and were processed solely in the amygdala.

Maybe there was a chance the two could have bonded if Qayum had interpreted Umati's gestures differently. There was a chance she could have been on a different side in the promotion discussion if she had recognized how her feminist narratives were at play.

No one can objectively know all the facts or make a judgment as, in a way, our individual realities are constructed in our minds. Qayum's former colleagues were not different characters in a movie. Rather, they were all watching and acting in different movies - comedies, tragedies, thrillers, and more. Each living out their own unique movie plot.

Besides, it is very difficult, if not impossible, for us to see the flaws in our perspective. It is much easier for us to see the faults of others. This is because the pre-frontal cortex spends significant resources in defending our actions and constructing stories that portray us in a better light than others.

A study on **self-serving bias** found that people are more likely to remember their own good deeds than their bad deeds. We are more likely to have stories that give us credit for our successes and blame others or circumstances for our failures.

All of this pre-wiring of our brain is out of our control, so when the sages ask us to control the mind, how can one succeed at it?

If knowledge alone was enough, then Qayum could have questioned her narrative and overcome the heartache it brings her, as she keeps up with brain research and finds it engrossing. There must be some unexplored avenue where answers await her arrival.

Qayum gets up from the rock and starts walking back to the cottage, trying to think only of her breath as it moves in and out. With each deep inhale, she perks up. As she approaches the cottage at the end of her run, the sun rides high, painting the cottage windows golden.

Inside, scents of freshly brewed coffee and sizzling butter waft through the cozy cottage kitchen as Qayum whips up a fluffy omelet. Following her meal, she runs her fingers across the weathered spines of books, carefully selecting a tale for the 11:30 reading.

The faint cries of seagulls through the open window remind her of the tranquil present.

Chapter 6: Perspectives

Qayum arrives at the library a few minutes before 11 am, wearing her old trusted blue dress paired with a golden cardigan and a broad, toothy smile. She greets the librarian, who points her to the children's section on the southwest corner of the first floor. A table is set up for the books alongside her poster.

The library is a beautiful modern building with large windows that brighten the interiors. Bean bags and cozy chairs populate the reading area. The walls are tastefully decorated with posters and murals. On this Saturday morning, the library is abuzz with activity. People browse the shelves while librarians assist patrons.

Qayum carefully unpacks boxes of her latest book, "The Adventures of A Squirrel," and displays them on the table, alongside bookmarks, posters, and an array of other whimsical trinkets bearing the now beloved bushy-tailed protagonist squirrel. She is nervously excited as parents and children start gathering around.

Watching the youthful wonder in their wide eyes, she contemplates her own relentless career climb - decades lost scaling corporate summits seeking validation from credentials and applause. Her family traditions had oriented her fixation outward on titles, wealth accumulation, and prestige as the pinnacle of achievement. Now, writing books themed around finding happiness is a reflection of her resolve to steer children towards a more balanced path. She hopes to nourish inner resilience through the importance of lasting friendships and everyday generosities.

Promptly at 11:30 a.m., Qayum introduces herself to the children and takes them through the book's main plotline. Then, she delves into the chapter she has chosen for the day: "Cracking the Happiness Nut." In this chapter, the squirrel sits atop a massive bounty of fruits, nuts, cakes, and pastries she had acquired on a treasure hunt adventure in the previous chapter of the book.

As Qayum reads, she brings the story to life, spellbinding her young audience. The squirrel possesses everything she ever desired, yet a persistent sense of boredom and unhappiness shadows her. Despite attempting various pursuits like playful chases, reading books, and outings to the park, the squirrel's search for happiness remains elusive.

The children sit spellbound as Qayum's narration transports them into the forest, where a serendipitous encounter awaits. *"Perched on a branch sits a great horned owl, tufts of feathers sprouting from his head. His large, unblinking eyes gaze at the squirrel as he hums a gentle tune.*

"Why are you so happy?" asks the curious squirrel.

"Because I have everything I need." responds the owl in a deep hushed tone.

"But I, too, have all I need," counters the squirrel, "and still, I am unhappy and constantly bored."

"In that case, you are looking for the wrong thing," advises the owl. "Happiness is not something you stumble upon; it's something you create."

"How do I create happiness?" inquires the curious squirrel.

"By being thankful for what you have and helping others be happy too," explains the owl patiently. "There are so many ways to do this that could be uniquely yours."

The squirrel reflects on the owl's words. She realizes her earlier ideas about happiness have led her down the wrong path. She has been too focused on her own wishes and has forgotten how important it is to appreciate what she has and also care for her friends.

The squirrel takes the owl's advice, expressing gratitude for the simple pleasures in her life—her family and friends, her tree, and her acorns. Being thankful becomes her daily ritual. Each morning, as she wakes up, she whispers, "Thank you for this beautiful day, for my home in the tree, for my cozy bed crafted from dry leaves, and…"

As the story unfolds, Qayum detects a flicker of restlessness among her younger audience. She pauses, radiates a warm smile, establishes eye contact across the room, and poses a question: "Does anybody have more ideas on how to practice gratitude?"

Enthusiastically, hands shoot up, and the children eagerly share their thoughts. An animated discussion ensues, with Qayum expressing appreciation for each suggestion. After all ideas have been explored, she resumes reading.

"During their chasing games, the squirrel discovers ways to offer kind words to her playmates. As the squirrel helps friends, her eyes shine, and her tail swishes joyfully. By bringing small smiles to others, she discoveres how to make her own happiness."

The book once again serves as a platform for inquisitive young minds to engage in a dialogue, exploring strategies to bring joy to those around them.

Resuming her storytelling, Qayum says, *"One fateful day, the squirrel hears a scary noise as she returns from the park. She looks up and spots a big, mean cat chasing a tiny, frightened mouse.*

The squirrel's heart pounds as she calls out to the cat, diverting his attention. The cat starts chasing the nimble squirrel as she expertly navigates the branches. After reaching high up in a redwood, the squirrel gazes around proudly, having led the mouse to safety.

In this act of bravery and kindness, the squirrel not only saves the mouse but also gains a new friend—thus creating another path to happiness."

The young audience erupts in applause, celebrating the squirrel's triumph. As the hour comes to an end, the children eagerly line up to secure not only copies of her book but also squirrel-themed trinkets.

Qayum is overjoyed to connect with her readers, signing books and immersing in heartfelt conversations. The librarian introduces her to a volunteer who provides invaluable assistance in managing the expanding crowd.

With the library's closing at 6 p.m., the book signing event draws to a close. Qayum is left with a sense of fulfillment and a rumbling stomach. The day has been a resounding success, and she holds close the precious moments spent sharing her passion for storytelling with eager young minds.

Now, Qayum's thoughts turn to her plans to meet an old friend and classmate, Ruhi, for drinks and dinner at a local Californian cuisine restaurant. Exhausted from all the talking and yet excited to meet her friend, Qayum makes her way to the car

Upon entering a brightly lit room, neatly organized with tables draped in gleaming white tablecloths, she spots Ruhi seated at the window overlooking the winery. Ruhi looks stunning in her short black dress and neatly partitioned straight black hair.

As soon as they spot each other, both Qayum and Ruhi break into a joyful and soft squeal of excitement. They share a warm and tight hug before taking their seats and facing each other. It's only been a few months since their last meeting, and they have stayed connected over the phone with updates on each other lives.

Their friendship goes back nearly 30 years, originating during their college days as young, aspiring engineers. Both were driven and competitive, with one consistently on top of the class. What brought them closer was their willingness to go the extra mile and hold informal study sessions to help their fellow struggling coursemates grasp important concepts.

Interestingly, neither of them had chosen engineering willingly; their parents had made that career decision for them. In the 90s, India offered limited opportunities, and they followed their parents' wishes. After graduation, Ruhi entered an arranged marriage and subsequently moved to the US with her husband.

For nearly 15 years, Ruhi thrived in the tech industry. Still, as time passed, she grew dissatisfied with the fact that the tech industry is seen as meritocratic when people are marginalized based on their gender and background. Feeling a strong urge to make a meaningful impact, she ventured into her own business—a thriving online tutoring service. The platform features educational videos catering to middle and high school students across various subjects.

Ruhi's final position in the tech industry was with a security startup that was the darling of Silicon Valley investors at the time. This company had completely revolutionized the cloud security sector, which was precisely what the market demanded at the time. As a senior leader in the marketing team, Ruhi found herself in the company of Joel, who had joined around the same time. The two often shared car rides to work.

Joel had come from a leading another security company, but he was displeased to find himself at the same grade level as Ruhi. During their drives to the city, he never missed a chance to boast about how this startup had pleaded for his recruitment, offering him a salary even higher than the CEO's. Joel was determined to seize control of the entire team and sought Ruhi's support in his ambitions. However, Ruhi tactfully shifted the conversation to upcoming product releases and launch plans, avoiding any confrontation.

Unbeknownst to Ruhi, Joel viewed her as a formidable rival to overcome. Her new messaging was very popular across demand generation, service renewals, and investor relations.

As Joel had predicted, changes soon started occurring in the company, leading to the removal of their boss. However, Joel's dream of becoming the boss himself was shattered when the chief marketing officer (CMO) decided to hire an external replacement.

The next time Joel and Ruhi spoke, he launched into a tirade, complaining about how much he had sacrificed for the company and how unappreciated he felt. Unwilling to give his ego a false boost or hurt him with her true opinion, Ruhi chose to remain silent.

During the company holiday party, as Ruhi was introducing her husband to her colleagues, she ran into Joel. "Hello, Joel," she said politely, "where is your wife? I was looking forward to meeting her."

His reply was dry and disdainful, revealing his deeply ingrained sexist attitude. "My wife is at home taking care of my four children," he quipped dismissively, moving on to shake hands with Ruhi's husband. An uncomfortable silence followed as Joel seemed to revel in the awkwardness he had created, staring them down with an air of superiority.

After the encounter, Ruhi's husband couldn't help but express his discomfort, remarking, "That was unpleasant."

Shortly after the New Year began, the team got a new manager. Sean was a young, blond individual with an eager-to-please demeanor. At the first team meeting, he announced that he wanted to connect with each team member individually and asked them to schedule a lunch meeting on his calendar.

Ruhi was the last to arrange the one-on-one meeting and opted for the food truck conveniently located down the street. They walked together, joined the line to order their wraps, and then took a seat on a bench under the shade of a large tree. However, the wraps turned out to be quite messy to eat, and the day's heat made it a bit uncomfortable to be outside.

The flow of their conversation seemed somewhat stilted, and Ruhi couldn't shake the sense of uneasiness between them. Despite this, two things stayed with her long after her meeting with Sean: his admiration for Joel's choice of venue - a beautiful, chic sit-down place by the bay and Sean's ambitious plan as the new VP to streamline the team by cutting some positions and hiring new people of his choosing. Sean viewed this approach as a sign of a strong leader and in alignment with the efficiency principles discussed in the recent leadership offsite.

When Sean unexpectedly placed Ruhi on probation, she was shocked and demanded an explanation for this sudden decision. Sean's response was far from satisfactory, as he coldly retorted, "If you were doing your job right, why would your colleague take me out for a long lunch just to highlight everything you are doing wrong?"

Determined to get to the bottom of the matter, Ruhi pressed Sean to reveal the colleague's identity. However, he remained evasive, saying he couldn't disclose that information. But Ruhi's intuition was sharp, and she directly asked if Joel had undermined her during that lunch meeting. Sean's facial expressions gave him away, confirming her suspicions.

Though one mere mortal marked for elimination by a formidable schemer, she resolved to sound defiance. Ruhi knew inaction would only cause her deeper despair. Poised with quiet courage, she decided to consult legal counsel and sent a formal notice to the company detailing her intent to challenge the unjust probation.

Following the notice, the company went into a whirlwind of activity. The CMO was seen marching toward the CEO's office while others hurried into urgent meetings. And throughout it all, Joel had an unsettling smirk on his face, as if enjoying the chaos.

The company responded to the escalating situation by bringing in a third party to conduct a survey aimed at addressing concerns related to diversity and workplace culture. Given the circumstances, they swiftly removed Sean from his position, and Joel was appointed as the acting VP.

Joel fulfilled his dream all on his own. Recognizing Sean's inexperience and vulnerability to manipulation, he saw an opportunity, and a strategy began forming in his mind. To execute it, he fabricated reasons to eliminate Ruhi's position and actively assisted Sean in developing the probation plan. Sean welcomed the help, as it conveniently aligned with his plan. What also helped them is that Ruhi did not fit the stereotypical image of a marketing leader, being both ethnically distinct and a woman, which made her stand out in their so-called 'leader club'.

Joel correctly predicted that Ruhi wouldn't back down without a fight, but he meticulously ensured that nothing could be traced back to him, leaving Sean to bear the consequences alone. With himself as the acting VP, Joel predicted Ruhi would want to give up and seek opportunities elsewhere.

In one master stroke, Joel had successfully eliminated both Sean and Ruhi, securing his position as acting VP and removing any competition or threats he perceived from Ruhi.

Despite how others interpreted the turn of events, Ruhi chose to make peace with the situation and even found humor in it. She jokingly said, "I'm grateful for Joel's nastiness. Without it, I'd still be on that exhausting tech industry's mouse wheel. I have a more meaningful life as my own boss now."

Ruhi exemplifies the wisdom found in Buddha's parable of two arrows. The first arrow represents the inevitable suffering we all face fairly consistently throughout life. The second arrow symbolizes the self-inflicted torment that comes from our response to the first arrow. This distress from the second arrow is absolutely optional and can be entirely avoided.

While Ruhi has a knack for dodging the second arrow, Qayum seems to cling to it - unwilling to let go of her unjust past. Despite the freedom to pursue her passion, she has managed to create a steady source of her own misery. In objective terms, her current life of sharing her love for stories with young, inquisitive minds is far superior to the one she left behind.

Meanwhile, Ruhi's reaction to her situation is to capitalize on whatever fate has thrown her way. Leveraging her Indian background, she set up an offshore operation to scale content creation for her online tutorial platform. She called in favors she'd extended over the years. She navigated new hurdles with sustained focus, never allowing herself to look back with regret or be consumed by 'what-if' or "if-only" scenarios. Her key resources for sidestepping the second arrow were self-love, can-do confidence, and fully living in the present moment.

In this moment the server interrupts the reverie as he hands them both a menu. The two brilliant women have been watching the changing colors of the winery from their window-side table as the sun disappears on the horizon. As they slowly resurface from private ponderings, the bustling dining room takes shape once more—the lilt of saxophones in tune with the clings of crystal glasses toasting under strings of fairylights.

Ruhi looks back at Qayum and asks with genuine curiosity, "How was the session at the library?"

"It was a great success," responds Qayum with a broad smile, snapping back to the present moment.

They both study the menu and discuss what to order. Ruhi decides on the Barigoule of Autumn Vegetables, and Qayum opts for the Artichoke and Fontina Cheese Ravioli. Agreeing to share their dishes, they decide on a bottle of rich, velvety Cabernet Sauvignon, a choice that promises to pair beautifully with the intricate flavors of their meal.

While waiting for their food to arrive, the ladies reminisce about their engineering days, laughing again at the old jokes, awkward professors, and, of course, those absurd yet endearing student characters encountered over years of relentless study sessions.

Their tour through memories fades as Ruhi, seemingly attuned to Qayum's thoughts, shifts the conversation. "Do you still agonize over the tech industry that was unkind, almost hostile to us?"

Just then, the server walks in with their food and extra plates for sharing. They dig into their dishes, savoring the exquisite flavors of the local produce. Between devouring the flavors bursting on their plates, both women express heartfelt gratitude for their life in California amid the bounty of its farms and vineyards.

Qayum studies her friend intently and admires her unwavering positivity towards life. Then, putting it to the test, she prepares to answer the temporarily suspended question. "Look at us," she begins, her tone contemplative, "two women who were the best in our class and excelled as technologists. Why could we not attain leadership positions in Silicon Valley? It cannot just be the fact that we are women. Other women like Umati have made it big. So, where did we fail?"

Ruhi's face is still calm as she responds, "We did not learn to play the game of self-preservation and self-promotion. We cared too much about the company's growth, technological innovations, and our peers, rather than pushing our own agenda."

They sit chewing in contemplative silence once more, absorbing the implications of Ruhi's words. Then Ruhi adds, "We have always prioritized family and home responsibilities. It's ingrained in us, part of our upbringing. You can say it's unfair, but, we do enjoy our roles as wives and mothers, don't we?"

Nodding slowly, Qayum acknowledges, "Our family is a source of consistent joy, and our responsibilities have been a priority, shaping our choices. While our male counterparts bonded over drinks and informal events after work, we had to rush home for pickups and preparing meals. It isolated us from the informal circles where valuable connections were often forged. It's disheartening to see the tech industry's lack of true inclusivity and support. There's so much showmanship to display inclusion, but where it matters, they have failed…" Her voice trails off into a sigh, "They have failed to include us."

"No, yaar, Don't you see? We are the fortunate ones who managed to escape the rat race," Ruhi says with a joyful laugh, trying to lift Qayum's spirits. "We have great lives, you and I, so why does the past matter now?"

This is the very question that has been gnawing at Qayum. "It should not! But it does, and I do not know why. I am trying to figure that out," she confides.

Ruhi winks playfully at Qayum, "Let's see if the chocolate mousse can help with your investigation," she suggests, then waves to the server to place the order.

The anticipation of the delicious dessert brings smiles to both their faces as they sit in silence, cherishing each other's company.

A new thought in Qayum's mind asserts, "It's your ego," as the divine chocolate mousse delights her taste buds.

"What is ego," counters another murmur still in her head. Qayum decides to ignore the voices for the time being and instead brings her complete attention back to the moment, savoring the warmth of her friend.

With a final embrace, she bids Ruhi goodbye and embarks on the drive back to her quaint cottage in the hills. The leftover food and wine from their scrumptious meal are safely tucked in her car's trunk.

Back in the cabin, she swiftly goes through her nightly rituals of changing, brushing, and moisturizing. Then, she settles onto her bed, sitting cross-legged, enveloped by the comforting embrace of solitude.

Qayum sinks into a trance-like state, focusing on her breath, much like a radio tuning into the frequencies and energies of the universe.

She is attuned to the vast expanse of wisdom that permeates existence, recalling how, in the past, those inner voices have provided guidance.

"I am ready to learn more about my ego to be free of its dictates," she breathes into the breeze. "Guide me."

The moonlight casts its gentle glow, creating a mystical ambiance around her. The crickets' soft chorus accompanies her in the invocation mantra:

Oṃ

Asato mā sad gamaya |

Tamaso mā jyotir gamaya |

Mṛtyor mā umṛtaṃ gamaya |

Oṃ śāntiḥ śāntiḥ śāntiḥ | |

Lead us from unreal to real

Lead us from darkness to light

Lead us from (the cycle of) death to immortality

Lead us to peace, peace, peace![12]

---

[12] The purifying prayer recited for the well-being of self and humanity is from Brihadaranyaka Upanishad, which was composed about the 6th-7th century BCE and is a part of Yajur Veda. The prayer recited in Sanskrit creates powerful vibrations in the body.

Chapter 7: Unveiling Prakruti

Back in the other realm, beyond the tangible, Sakshi, Maya, and Prakruti have a sprawling view of the grassy meadows sweeping down to sapphire lakes. They are the conductors and narrators of the imminent enlightening revelations.

This isn't an ordinary broadcast, the kind transmitted through radios or sound waves. Instead, it is an internal communion, a resonance tapped into through the intricate workings of the human mind.

To authentically grasp its core message, one must dispel the clutter of earthly distractions, harmonizing their consciousness with the universe's subtle energies. These insights often appear as inspirations during moments of introspective daydreaming, people-watching, exercising, traveling, or in the intense focus of a task.

Maya and Prakruti's anticipation shifts towards Sakshi as she addresses her companions and extends her words to all sentient beings in the universe, "We've discussed techniques to navigate the challenges from being a slave to your physical senses and brainy pleasures. Today, let us explore the subtler yet equally powerful master that controls you—your egoic identity.

Suffering arises from the ego's needs—the hankering to feel valued, distinct, and a contributing element of society. This persistent sense of 'I' drives you to chase recognition and accolades and to carve out a distinct presence.

It is said that the sole shared thread between serial killers, super successful people, influential leaders, and everyone else is the deeply-ingrained need to be acknowledged by the world and ideally be admired."

Sensing the perspective may still seem abstract for some, Sakshi's gaze meets Maya's, inviting her to elucidate further.

Maya takes over, "Appreciation kindles profound joy. Sometimes, even more than the sensory delights of the physical world like a warm bath or cheesy pizza. It acknowledges our unique existence and entices our ego, fueling pursuits of societal stature, power, and titles.

We adorn ourselves, shed weight, and acquire possessions, often to craft social media personas or leave impressions at events, sculpting an image palatable for the world to adore.

Within our thinking minds, we grasp our individual insignificance. Our existence is but a fleeting moment in the grand scheme of time, spanning a mere 80-90 years in contrast to the vast expanse of billions of years in the universe's history.

We are a mere whisper in the cosmic symphony. The relentless march of the world continues, unaffected by the passage of celebrated leaders or brilliant minds. Our absence would scarcely cause a ripple beyond our closest circles.

Yet, the hunger for meaning and importance persists—a ceaseless force propelling us forward in constant pursuit of what others might envy - more money, power, strength, philanthropy, beauty, and on and on.

Our sense of self-importance feeds like a ravenous creature, gorging endlessly upon the world's offerings. With each morsel of praise and flattery, it grows increasingly insatiable and fragile. Even minor criticisms can fatally wound it, causing us significant pain. When our ego takes a hit, we feel real threats to our very existence.

Yet, criticism and adversity serve a vital role in revealing our blind spots and nurturing better versions of ourselves. Much like the gold ore that needs to burn through fire to become purified gold. So why avoid such catalysts that distill our patience and wisdom? Why not actively seek situations or people that test our character's resilience and push its qualities to their limits? Why chase praises that have nothing to offer?"

Maya's words reverberate through the crystalline mountain air. She surveys the terrain of grassy meadows along the deep blue lake, absently brushing her fingers through the wildflowers at her feet. Their velvety petals carry the sun's lingering warmth.

After allowing time for her message's gravity to permeate, she continues, "When we crave approval or aspire to be respected by others, we allow their opinions to influence our actions, behavior, and thoughts. In a way, we can be expertly maneuvered through flattery, particularly if it is well-delivered. In the pursuit of self-importance, we are now serving countless new masters!

We also relish recounting our tales, basking gloriously in our own spotlight, and reveling indulgently in stories of our own greatness. These actions may not necessarily endear us to others, but they certainly bestow us with a sense of gratification. Yet, the contentment derived from ego elevation is only temporary…"

"… similar to the intoxicating yet ephemeral joy derived from sensory pleasures, the exhilaration stemming from ego inflation inevitably proves short-lived." Prakruti adds, rounding off Maya's statement.

"Bravo!" Sakshi exclaims, "You have articulated it brilliantly! This is the third master who unwittingly claims human allegiance. The first master, of course, is the physical body itself, with its sensory demands, and the second master is the intellect.

Prakruti poses the obvious question, "How can individuals escape their innate predisposition to be influenced by praise or disapproval?"

Sakshi responds, "You can start by envisioning the ego as an intangible sensory organ, a construct of the mind. You may already recognize that the human body comprises a wide array of entities that perform all the necessary functions.

These outcomes are attributed to the Ego for the sake of coherence and simplicity. For instance, when someone remarks, 'I see a flower,' it is the eyes that have captured the light, the visual cortex that has constructed the image, and the memory function that assigns the name.

The ego then appropriates the credit for the work of these diverse entities and declares triumphantly, 'I see the flower!'

It weaves self-aggrandizing narratives about a person's identity. As you begin to perceive the ego for what it truly is, you can begin the process of being free from its grip.

Each time the ego claims credit or takes refuge in blame, it obscures reality. When an athlete says 'I' performed these unparalleled feats,' there was no contribution made by the ego or the 'I.' All the work was done through coordinated muscles, rhythmic heartbeats, oxygen-rich breaths, and more. When a scientist or mathematician has solved a complex problem, the accomplishment is a result of the intricate synaptic dance within the brain.

By consistently practicing recognizing the truth and disregarding the ego's assertions of winnings and failures, you can be free from the pressures that push you to constantly seek approval and evade criticism."

Maya is mindful of the audience's perspective and presents the ultimate problem, "Dissociating oneself from the ego is no simple feat. If we cannot see ourselves as the doer, then what are we?"

Sakshi continues, "You are the purest form of awareness that resides within a vessel with three distinct components[13]. Firstly, there's the physical body—a tangible vessel housing the organs and senses to enable physical interaction with the world. It is simply everything physical in your body.

Then, there's the subtle body—a realm that encompasses the mind's expanse and vital energies. Within this realm are thoughts, emotions, and intellect that govern your perception and responses to the world. This is where the illusions of the material realm take shape.

Lastly, consider the causal body[14]—the seed or the origin of both the physical and subtle body. It has no other functions beyond holding the potential state for the other two bodies. It also holds the imprints of past conducts and future potentials."

---

[13] Three Bodies and Five Sheaths, is an essential principle in Indian philosophy, especially Yoga, Advaita Vedanta, Tantra, and Shaivism.

[14] Is there a relationship between the causal body in ancient philosophy and the modern discovery of genes? Could causal body be our genes?

At the end of her words, Sakshi shifts into a reflective state, her aura radiating tranquility. Her words linger in the air like a gentle breeze.

Maya humbly seeks further clarification to facilitate a clearer understanding for their audience across various realms in the universe, "The concepts of the physical and subtle bodies seem more accessible to human comprehension. However, the elusive causal body might seem beyond mortal grasp. Besides, how do the insights into these layers of bodies help us get liberated from the human ego?"

Sakshi's eyes remain closed, and her smile is a reflection of deep appreciation for Maya's efforts in simplifying the discourse. "Patience, my dear." Her gaze is now directed at the magnificent Banyan tree, its ancient branches adorned with hanging roots—an embodiment of timelessness. "Observe that venerable Banyan tree," Sakshi gestures toward the majestic spectacle several centuries old.

"Would you agree that the potential of that enormous tree was always in this tiny seed?" she says, holding out her palm with a tiny seed less than a centimeter wide. "Even as the seed remains unsprouted or as it was sprouting or when it was a tiny sapling at risk of being stepped on or blown away. The potential of this gigantic creature remains unchanged even as its physical structure underwent many changes. This dormant power is held in the causal body."

Maya's expression is filled with curiosity as she jumps in, "So, are you suggesting that everything that this tree was meant to be was already predetermined?"

"No," Sakshi's voice is unwavering, "nothing is predetermined. Let us not mistake this potential for destiny. The path a seed takes to become a majestic Banyan tree is influenced by the soil's and water's nourishment, the sun's warmth, and the gentle touch of the wind. Not every seed fulfills its utmost potential, as the culmination of its potential is determined by the mystical play of nature." Sakshi says, inspiring awe for the forces of nature. Then proceeds to introduce Prakruti, the very embodiment of the primal creative, sustaining, and destructive forces of nature.

As Prakruti steps into the narrator's role, her words ripple outward to reach all sentient beings, "Let us begin with venturing deeper into the narrative of that very seed—the silent bearer of the magnificent Banyan tree's promise. It was I who crafted this potential and organized the myriad conditions necessary for its realization.

Contemplate the latent potential dwelling within your causal body and the inherent capacities within your physical and cerebral faculties. Do you truly own them, or are they manifest through forces far greater, far longer lasting than your individual existence?

For a moment, imagine trying to operate your body - regulating the heartbeat, the breath, and the countless processes of digestion, along with the nodes and glands that sustain your being. Could any mortal mind consciously orchestrate that complexity underlying life's miracle? Surely, such mastery extends well beyond the realm of individual control.

What is more astonishing is that not all the living cells in your body were created by specifications provided by your causal body. You know these other creations as microbes. The trillions of microorganisms that live in your body outnumber your living human cells by 10 to 1. They enable your survival by carrying out critical functions that ensure your immunity, digestion, excretion, and even your moods.

Picture this intricate collaboration between you and the microbial realm, an alliance that highlights the marvelous depth of nature's craftsmanship within you. As you reflect upon this web of existence, it becomes increasingly evident that your body, mind, and intellect are not possessions you own. Rather, they belong to the cosmic treasury. They are instruments on loan, merely having a brief existence. "

I would like to pause the broadcast for a trivia. You probably already know that the word 'persona' originally referred to the mask worn by actors in Roman theater. Over time, it came to be used to refer to a person's public image or role in society, which, in its own way, is a subtle mask. Here,

Prakruti is reminding us, perhaps, of the wisdom known and forgotten through generations. The body, mind, and intellect are only a mask worn by the true self for a short performance in this lifetime.

Shifting back to the transmission, Prakruti continues her explanation: "So, when actions arise through the body, mind, and intellect of your being, they're not just individual accomplishments but a mere note in the eternal song.

The universe has lent you the triad bodies as tools to participate in its masterpiece performance. Nature originates the need for action, and it is nature that conducts the activities.

To grasp this idea, let us look at a mundane example from your everyday life to visualize nature's symphony in motion. Nature triggers needs within you – hunger, thirst, curiosity – igniting the urge to act. Let's take the example of hunger. It's nature's way of nudging you to find sustenance, perhaps urging you to gather or hunt.

As you respond to nature's cues, you rely on the tools nature has provided – your body's agility, your mind's ingenuity, and your intellect's discernment. These tools are nature's gifts, aiding you in fulfilling the very needs it has sparked. From the initial stirrings of hunger to the gratification of a meal, it's all part of nature's choreography.

The role nature has assigned to you could be that of the Olympic gold medal-winning gazelle or the earthworm enjoying the slow life enriching the soil.

It is futile to desire a different life since that is already predetermined. You can instead find ways to excel at your assigned role."

As Prakruti pauses, Sakshi gracefully takes the lead, guiding the discourse toward its conclusion.

With a compassionate poise, she raises a thought-provoking question, "If you acknowledge that you don't own your body, intellect, and mind and that you bear no responsibility for even a single breath of life, then how can you perceive yourself as the sole architect of your life's success or failure?"

In response, the resonant chants of countless rishis fill Sakshi's broadcast frequencies. Their collective voices create healing vibrations across the cosmos.

Sung in the ancient tongue of Sanskrit, these verses generate harmonious resonances that vibrate through the very fabric of every being. The vibrations convey:[15]

---

[15] From Bhagwad Gita 13.30 - Only they see, who see that all actions are performed by prakruti alone, and that the Self is actionless. See appendix.

"In the cosmic tournament's expanse,
Prakruti governs life's game of chance.
All actions, every victory and defeat,
Are by Nature's design, and she owns every feat.
Surrender ego's claim, and you shall see
Your true self will be set free."

Sakshi draws the broadcast to a close, "With awakened observation, one recognizes they navigate happenings arising randomly, employing the traits and capacities bestowed by nature.

Outcomes simply reflect the complex interplay of these factors. Suffering springs from ego-woven tales of personal authorship over life's outcomes - invented narratives of conquests, rewards you feel owed.

Recognizing Prakruti's detached rhythms liberates you to engage fully in each temporary dance, unmoved by applause or critique echoing when the music ends."

Chapter 8: Dissolving Ego

Time in Qayum's world has a relentless tempo. As she packs up her belongings on the last day of her California tour, she reflects on how quickly the time has passed.

Her days have whirled by in a flurry of book readings and signings; her evenings were steeped in meditation, seeking a path out of the fog of confusion and ignorance.

Every evening, she dedicated some time to introspection, examining why she clung to her past. Why harbor resentment?

Stoics preached that power, or the hunger for it, breeds a particular type of ruthlessness. Therefore, we must expect to encounter evil, immorality, and deceit in the world and prepare ourselves for it.

Questioning the existence of immoral or evil individuals is akin to questioning the laws of nature itself[16]. Just as light requires dark and warmth needs cold, kindness necessitates cruelty to exist. One extreme helps define the other. Such dualities arise inevitably as part of existence.

These contemplations lead her to appreciate the simple joys in her present life, particularly the faces of the children, as they discover the magic in her stories. She feels grateful for

---

[16] From Meditations by Marcus Aurelius.

their imaginative minds, wide eyes filled with wonder, and contagious laughter still ringing in her memory.

Months ago, she had been swept in the preparations with maps spread across the various tabs on her browser, dotted with the coastal towns of California, and her suitcase slowly filled with essentials and non-essentials. Prakashay's emails and itinerary reminders had been a constant presence in her inbox, building excitement and anticipation.

During this past week, she had exceeded both her and Prakashay's expectations by selling all the books she was carrying with her. Finding herself with no books left to sell to the readers she met in Half Moon Bay's library, she had called her dependable agent, Prakashay. Together, they crafted a unique solution: a special online code that would enable her signed copies to be delivered directly to those attending the reading. This inventive workaround allowed her to continue to connect with her readers, even after the unexpected success had left her without physical books.

With the final readings and signing sessions complete, she finds herself in a reflective mood. Today marks the end of her road trip, one-third of her three-week adventure.

Qayum starts this day of leisure with freshly brewed hot lavender tea and settles into a chair on the porch, facing the uninterrupted expanse of the ocean. She feels the warmth of the tea as it travels through her neck and chest, warming her stomach, while the cool breeze from the sea gently caresses her face. The dualities of life drive life's experiences.

Turning inward, Qayum traces her buried pain, seeking its source. The trail leads to wounded self-esteem, entwined with her professional identity and others' perceptions. As she tries to disentangle herself, to her dismay, she discovers that she values nothing within herself outside of the worth ascribed to her by the opinions and actions of others. So, without someone's external indication - praise, reward, promotion, title - she has no way of knowing what she may be truly worth.

An overlooked yet critical role of the Stoic virtues is to instill strong personal values that anchor us. When we cultivate unshakable values within - such as courage, compassion, hardwork, moderation, and justice- we become immune to the fickle opinions or malintent of others. Much like a moral compass, these intrinsic virtues guide us through puzzling and perilous travels. By consciously embedding noble qualities as our steadfast gauge of our own right and wrong, we develop a stubborn resilience.

As she contemplates reinforcing this inner fortitude, she discovers an insatiable sense of entitlement to receive positive reinforcement from everyone around. Qayum believes she has earned everyone's unconditional adoration through her amazing work. This realization unveils a deep-seated contradiction within her: a yearning for recognition and fairness juxtaposed with the knowledge that external validation should not define her worth. What, then, is the outcome of her good work?

Qayum's thoughts turn to her values and role at work, "My role was to manage the product lifecycle, and I left no stone unturned to make it succeed.

Yet the grief lingers like an open wound. Why? Is it because there was not enough appreciation? Or is it a sense of failure from being laid off? Or was it bitterness around plans thwarted by Umati? Or the inability to influence the promotion committee?"

Qayum's mind flashes back to her early years, filled with recognition and praise that stoked a fire to strive harder and reach higher. She had been addicted to success, a relentless pursuit that fueled her pride. Like a powerful opioid, each triumph delivered only quick elation before wearing off, leaving her to compulsively chase the next dose of glory.

A realization dawns on her, more like a forceful push from her inner self. "I have been obsessed with winning, drawing inspiration from the lives of those hailed as victors, and focusing on strategies to succeed. Even my failures were lessons to win another day. Striving for great outcomes has been fundamental to my sense of purpose, propelling me to nonstop action. It's why I studied so hard, helped others, and sought recognition. It defined who I was and my connection to the world. This attachment to my actions and their outcomes—it's been there all along, woven into the fabric of my being. My psyche persists in extracting endless external validation to fill the chasm of self-worth. I need the world to consistently appreciate me to replace my lack of inherent self-love or feed my larger-than-life ego?"

Tears roll down her cheeks as the weight of these thoughts pushes the agony to the surface. Despite the raw ache in her heart, she persists in investigating its source within her.

Then, a new sensation develops, like something inside her has just tuned into another realm. The vibrations submerge her and transform into her thoughts. Although Qayum does not recognize the source of these vibrations as Prakruti, the message is clear in her mind.

"Contemplate the latent potential dwelling within your causal body and the inherent capacities within your physical and intellectual faculties. Do you truly own them, or are they manifestations of a grander design, surpassing the boundaries of your individual existence?

If you acknowledge that you don't own your body, intellect, and mind and bear no responsibility for even a single breath of life, how can you perceive yourself as the sole architect of your life's success or failure?"

Qayum's tears seem unstoppable. It is as if floodgates to an inner reservoir have just been breached. She closes her eyes and tries to focus on her breath as she deliberates, "I have no right to the fruits of my actions, yet they deeply affect me. These actions are not even completely my own; they are a product of the physical and intellectual capabilities and opportunities - all of which were given to me by the grace of creation or a flip of a coin!

The wind can make the leaves on a tree dance, and the rain can make the flowers bloom even when no one notices. So why this attachment to my deeds or their outcomes?" she questions.

All the haunting memories from her time in the tech world have been stored in high-definition. It's as if her mind has constructed a video archive, with each scene starring her wounded ego unwilling to forgive offenses against her self-image.

In the past, the slightest perceived attack to her pride whirred up the mental projector to life, replaying every single previous hurtful account in exhaustive detail. Try as she may, she could not switch it off. Even as she frantically tried tricks to distract herself, the cerebral surround-sound could not be silenced. Every frame a sting of humiliation, every voice a cruel reminder of her imperfections - replaying through the night into the early morning.

But today, rather than recoil from these memories, she steps courageously into the theater of the past. With a fresh perspective, she takes a front-row seat, ready to truly witness herself across varied episodes. Her objective today is to not flinch from moments scarring egoic pride nor avert her gaze from flashes of inadequacy, instead to merely observe without judgment. She signals for the show to begin.

The scene shifts to Qayum's first job. Initially, she had been terrified of taking customer calls, her anxiety compounded by a mentor who bore an undisguised disdain towards immigrants like her. One day, he snapped, "How would you like it if we came to your country and stole all your jobs?"

She'd felt humiliated then, made an outsider. But revisiting the memory now, in the backdrop of her new insights, Qayum observes it differently. She sees her mentor's insecurity - never traveling far from home, his father pushed out of the workforce as the manufacturing jobs shifted overseas. Now, he was scared to see Qayum's talent and was terrified of the prospect of losing his own job. He was not lashing out at Qayum, but at the potential change she represented.

Distancing herself from the hurt she had a much better perspective of the situation. Her heart was filled with compassion for that old mentor, and she not only forgave him instantly but also sent out wishes for his well-being.

Next on the playlist plays the scene where she was the only woman in the customer support org on the entire floor.

Upon hearing her high-pitched, accented voice, customers on the other end of the line would occasionally demand to talk to a "real engineer." She had to constantly prove her worth, suppressing emotional reactions to blatant discrimination.

The show in her mind then jumps forward to when she is in her boss's office, a performance review in her trembling hands with the words "needs improvement." She had been the top case closer for several months in a row, and now she is being told she needs to be assisting others on the team and not just work her own cases.

"I help anyone who asks me for help. Can you give me an example of someone I have not helped?" she asked, hurt and bewildered. Her manager's response was that it would not be easy for her male team members to ask a woman for help, so she should take the initiative.

"You're not being fair," Qayum contends. Undeterred, her boss pledges daily meetings to "help" her help others more. "But what about my own cases?" she protests. "Come early, stay late," he shrugs.

It was an impossible bind. Refuse and be fired. Spend all day aiding others, and her stats tank, prompting dismissal.

In Qayum's belief system, only the lazy or incompetent found themselves saddled with "improvement plans." She had been so proud of her skills and intellect. The humiliation of being put on such a plan was crushing to her. She had tried to keep the meeting with her boss a secret, but word had somehow already spread, turning her private shame into public embarrassment.

A few days later, one of her colleagues, Chris, pulled her aside. He confided that his uncle was the head of the support organization, a fact he'd rather keep under wraps. But he was concerned about the unjust way Qayum was being treated and wanted to help. Chris asked Qayum's permission to arrange a meeting with his uncle to challenge the "improvement plan."

Qayum had never imagined being able to stand up to management. Despite taking pride in her acumen and hard work, she was a nobody in the Valley—an immigrant who needed to keep her head down and work hard.

But Chris filled her with motivation, insisting she was the most exceptional engineer he had met and that her work spoke volumes. "There's nothing to be afraid of," he encouraged. "You shouldn't accept this injustice."

Through Chri's encouragement, she initiated an official investigation. Her manager was demoted soon after, and Qayum was promoted not once but twice that year.

Even though she had won the battle, she was badly scarred. Instead of focusing on Chris's kindness, her memory clung to the embarrassment she felt when placed on probation and

111

the long weeks and months of struggling to converse with her teammates.

Now, the entire scene replays in front of her, as it has countless times before. But this time, something's shifted. Every character and every action is an energy wave, interconnected and emanating from a single source. It's like watching a laser light show or a ballet, the intricate movements of negative and positive energies dancing in perfect synchrony. This dance of energies is a breathtaking spectacle. There are no victims and no victors. It is just the laws of the cosmos playing out in their own rhythm.

For the first time ever, Qayum can relive the incident without feeling any pain. In this interplay of forces, she discovers gratitude for her role and profound empathy for those who had harassed her. Governed by the immutable laws of karma and nature, they were merely fulfilling their part in the world's grand theater.

As one troubling memory fades, the next begins to play, and Qayum watches dispassionately. The next segment features Umati, Bimal, and Nandan all playing their temporary roles - not as villains or heroes but as fellow players in the short, twisty-turny production. The mind wants to know which one it should queue up next. Qayum responds with conviction, "They are all the same. Play them all, or don't play them. It makes no difference."

Her focus then shifts back to how Chris was inserted as a savior in her story. Was it all a part of nature's miraculous work? What prompted the innovative ideas that solved complex technical issues or inspired impactful customer presentations? Could she honestly claim credit for the remarkable projects she got the opportunity to work on?

She reflects on the many figures, like Chris, who had advocated for her and how her career appeared to be guided by some unseen force—sometimes leading her to peaks, other times into valleys. Her life in technology had been challenging, but it was never boring. Viewing her past through this new lens, she realizes there is no room for self-pity.

In contemplating these memories, a fresh understanding dawns upon Qayum. The narrative of her life is complex, but now, free from the shackles of her ego and entitlement, her journey seems extraordinarily exhilarating - she sees beauty now where she once saw only lack. With this newfound lucidity, she feels as if she's dissolving into her very core.

Time seems to stand still as Qayum's eyes lock onto the glimmering expanse of the ocean. She feels herself transform into a slow-moving wave, gradually closing in on the shore. Glancing around, she sees figures from her past as waves—some large, some small. Each is shaped by creation's whims. Some swell up to be speedy or splashy,

113

some are crowned with laces of froth, and yet others are unremarkable.

It would be futile for them to feel pride or shame for their size, shape, and speed as notwithstanding their temporary attributes, they will be merged back into the water. Swells of pride or troughs of disgrace hold no meaning in the currents of a fathomless, churning sea.

Magnificent surges, tiny ripples, every watery mound shares one destiny - to eventually crash onto the shore. Each of us will dissolve back into the sea, only to be born again. We are bound in the endless cycle of birth and death.

"Then who is the victor, and who is a failure?" she inquires out loud.

Her stomach responds with a loud growl. She checks her watch and realizes she's missed both breakfast and lunch. Nature sounding its drumbeat, summoning sustenance to nourish the mortal form.

Slipping into her comfy jeans, she ventures into a bustling eatery. She sits at the table, surrounded by the chatter and clatter of diners, relishing the newfound sense of detachment and appreciation of this world.

Her thoughts drift back to her revelations. There is a sense of lightness as if a weight has been lifted. Yet, she knows this feeling will soon be lost to the rigors of everyday life. It is evanescent, like the rainbow that slowly subdues into the blue sky; these realizations can be easily lost in the modern, active life's clouded gaze.

Like a recovered addict facing familiar triggers, there is a good chance she will soon feel pride in her work and relish the occasional praises until they turn into cravings. She must discipline her mind and remain unyielding if she is to make this newfound clarity a lasting state.

Without vigilant cultivation, these insights will fade to wisps of memories, deteriorate, and be washed away by the unceasing currents of daily routine and distractions.

Reflecting on the toolkit she had previously employed to conquer physical and sensory appetite, she wonders if the same principles could be applied to be free from ego. Her conclusion is unequivocal: "No, the permanent dissolution of my ego will require something far more potent.

I must find an unshakeable anchor for my identity. I am not the physical body, the thoughts, emotions, intellect, or even the ego that claims to be the doer of all actions. Then what am I?"

Chapter 9: Reinventing Faith

"Qay, Qay!" an unfamiliar voice calls out as Qayum is waiting at the check-in counter with her luggage. No one calls her Qay anymore. Qayum turns and sees her old friend Bhakti approaching. "BK! Is that really you?" she says in disbelief. Bhakti dashes towards her. They hold hands and smile in wonderment. They embrace awkwardly. "It's been nearly 35 years!" says Qayum, still in a state of happy shock.

When it is her turn at the airline counter, the attendant asks Qayum her destination. "Copenhagen," she replies. Bhakti whispers that she's also headed there and asks if they should try to sit together. "Yes!" Qayum bursts out enthusiastically. Bhakti hands the attendant her boarding pass. The attendant smiles, amused by the middle-aged women's unrealistic excitement about being reunited.

There is so much to catch up on, but neither knows where to begin. The last time they saw each other was at the high school graduation. Bhakti was already engaged to be married into a wealthy family in Kenya, as was tradition for merchant clans like hers.

With Bhakti sailing abroad and how complicated international calling was back then, they assumed they'd never reconnect. They said goodbyes. Their lives were heading in opposite directions: Bhakti would try to uphold traditions while Qayum was pursuing engineering to find independence.

After getting through security, the two friends find an airport bar and order Gin & Tonics. Over the din of the terminal, Bhakti asks, "How has life treated you so far?"

"No complaints," Qayum grins, taking a sip as memories stir. "Were you in Kenya or South Africa? Why are you in San Francisco? And headed to Copenhagen?"

Bhakti laughs affectionately, "You haven't changed one bit! Still the same boundless gusto as always. So wonderful to see you, Qay! I'd nearly forgotten this feeling in your presence - a breathless rush just keeping your pace!"

"And I love being with you—cool as a cucumber, without a care in the world," Qayum responds, relishing the moment in her dear friend's company.

Their drinks arrive, and they toast to serendipity for reuniting them. It's a wonderful feeling to rediscover an old, lost friend and feel your youthful self again.

After taking a sip of her drink, Bhakti begins, "I was here attending a family friend's wedding in Napa. What an incredible coincidence to run into you! Do you live in California now?"

Qayum: "Yes, for 27 years now! But first, tell me everything about your life from the time we last saw each other."

Bhakti: "It is quite a story. Do you remember I got married to Mihir soon after graduation?" Qayum affirms, and so Bhakti continues, "Well, his family has factories throughout Kenya—construction materials, grain packaging, heavy machinery. They've been there for generations.

Moving to Kenya changed my whole life. I lost touch with all my friends and family. Mombasa wasn't like Bombay—I couldn't just step out and meet people. I had to learn their ways and figure out how to fit into this new world. But Mihir has been very loving and supportive. We have two kids now. My son graduated from Oxford's business school and is being groomed to take over the family business. My daughter is following her passion for journalism.

I left Kenya and settled with my mother in Edinburgh about five years ago."

Qayum, with evident concern, asks, "Why did you leave Kenya? And what about Mihir?"

Bhakti's face darkens as she begins recounting the night of the home invasion. "It was about seven years ago. Mihir was out on a business trip to Europe. I was home with my daughter, getting ready for bed, when our house got broken into. The intruders were from some local gang. They seemed to know where everything valuable was hidden, even where

118

our safe was. But they did not know the code. I was beaten and thrown around as they demanded the code. I begged them to let me see my daughter first, to know she was okay.

My pleas centered solely on beholding my child one precious last time despite their continued brutality. Each suffocating chokehold plunged me into blackness. I'd claw back to pure terror, only to feel ruthless hands crushing my throat once more. The horror of that night is something I can never forget. I don't know how I am still alive." Bhakti looked up and tried to mask her grief by forcing on a smile.

Qayum is stunned into silence and then stammers, "Oh, BK! I'm so sorry - I had no idea something so awful was even possible! How is your daughter now?"

Mustering strength, Bhakti continued, "I was sure I was going to die that day. As I prepared myself to die, they finally gave me my daughter, and I gave them the code." A tear escaped on to her cheek.

Overwhelmed by Bhakti's story, Qayum sits in disbelief, staring at her friend. She studies the lines time has drawn on her beautiful and once flawless face and, leaning in, whispers, "You are so brave, BK! I am not sure someone else would have had the presence of mind or strength to stand against those men."

Bhakti carries on faintly, "You see why I had to leave Kenya? It was impossible to stay in that house again. Even after all the cleanup and restorations, I could still feel those men there. I could not fall asleep. We moved homes, but still, I found no peace in Kenya.

You know the worst part? It was one of our trusted staff who betrayed us. This is how the intruders knew Mihir and Keyur would not be home and where everything valuable in the house was kept. I even saw a hand-drawn map of the house in the clutches of one of the men and recognized the handwriting immediately."

Voice wavering, Bhakti reveals the painful circumstances behind the security breach. "It was a boy I'd recently hired into the household staff. He was in a dire situation when I found him in the streets, and I wanted to help him in some way. In the evenings, I would teach him to read and write. That's how I knew the hand that had drawn the map."

Qayum allows her tears to fall freely, feeling her friend's pain. Bhakti's experiences might as well have emanated from an alien world - marrying a stranger chosen by your family, having a household staff, taking a local from the streets into your own home, getting choked over and over again, and then living to tell the story. Every part of Bhakti's story highlights how vastly different their lives have become.

"Qay, your turn! Tell me your story," says Bhakti, sniffling and staring at Qayum with a curious smile.

Qayum has many more questions but doesn't want to prolong her friend's pain. She seizes the opportunity to steer the conversation. "Well, despite my hatred of calculus and Indian boys, I graduated with honors and even fell in love at Mumbai University. I escaped arranged marriage by coming to America - the land of dreams! I worked in Silicon Valley for a couple of decades, and now I'm a children's book author."

"That's awesome! But why leave tech?"

"Because it couldn't handle my genius!" Qayum says, attempting humor as tears brimmed her eyes. Perceiving emotions still raw, Bhakti redirects the conversation to a lighter fare, "Did you ever get married?"

"Yes! To my soulmate, Vatsal, I met at Mumbai University."

"An Inter-caste marriage?"

"It is even more shocking - he's Hindu!"

"No way!! How did you pull it off?"

"It's a long, complicated story full of surprises," Qayum says as the boarding is announced. They gather their belongings and line up, continuing to swap tidbits as they board.

Bhakti: "Do you still fast for Ramzan?"

Qayum: "Not anymore. After the Bombay blasts and subsequent riots, I lost faith in everything - Allah, Bhagwan, and God. You left before all that happened, but you must've read about it?"

"Yes, the 1993 Bombay blasts following the Babri Masjid demolition. It was terrible. But it wasn't the first time religious tensions have boiled over in India," Bhakti says, struggling to fit her bag into the overhead compartment.

Qayum slides to the window seat, pondering the insightful question. "The riots were my first encounter with such brutality as a young adult, and I was shocked to see the dark side of people. Do you remember Ahmed, who used to deliver eggs by bicycle? Fanatical men, fueled by religious hatred, broke his bike. When he returned on foot, they broke his eggs and beat him so severely that he ended up in the hospital.

Nobody knows exactly who these people were. Every Muslim-owned store in our community—be it a teakwood shop, a butchery, or a bakery—was destroyed. Even Faiz, who stitched our house curtains and mattresses - his shop was set ablaze. This is in our neighborhood, where Muslims were minorities. In other areas, Hindus faced similar horrors where they were outnumbered.

The riots had a lasting impact on everyone. Some endured physical harm, others mental anguish from being surrounded by fear and hatred. Everyone was preoccupied with exchanging horror stories from their localities.

Tension was evident in my engineering college. It felt like friends would suddenly stop talking when I came in. They were probably discussing atrocities against Hindus and wanted to spare me any embarrassment. I didn't feel spared, I felt abandoned."

Qayum pauses and stares out of the window. Below, the city lights sparkle, blurred at times by the wispy cloud cover drifting past. It is as if the starry sky has descended to now lie below them. The twinkling lights form a series of cryptic symbols interconnected through delicate golden & red threads of traffic.

Despite the years that have passed, the events from that pivotal period of her life remain fresh. She continues recounting her memories, "It wasn't a complete abyss of darkness and malice. Though the altruistic tales got overshadowed. In fact, most neighbors stood in solidarity with each other. They even painted their house nameplates blank, obscuring whether the household was Hindu or Muslim.

Young men took on patrol duties in the night, watching for approaching mobs of rioters, and our neighbors sheltered us whenever tensions flared up. However, the accounts of bravery and compassion were lost in the shuffle. The only stories that took hold were the ones depicting horror, circulating endlessly. They angered and polarized even the good, reasonable people.

After the riots, my friendships seemed unchanged on the surface, but invisible barriers had emerged. Those who once invited me to their temple visits stopped reaching out. I was just left with my dwindling circle of Christian friends. For the first time, I found myself mentally screening people based on their faith before calling them over to hang out. It was painful.

I blamed Allah, Bhagwan, and the deities I once revered for all the chaos. I stopped praying then. At home, during family prayer times, my participation was mechanical, a mere formality devoid of devotion. I remember just being angry and empty."

Bhakti intervenes, "I cannot believe you 'fired' God!? For things humans have done?"

"Do you not see how religious institutions are trying to control people with promises of heaven or threats of hell? So why would .." Qayum starts to explain.

Talking over, Qayum, agitated Bhakti, takes over, "Qay," she exclaims loudly and then softly adds, "You were my first glimpse of spirituality. When I sat with you in the Chapel, the Krishna Mandir, the Balaji temple, and even that under-construction Jain Temple - eyes closed - I felt the presence

124

of God. Sitting still, deeply focused on whatever sacred symbols stood before us, we found divinity! "

"We were kids, and kids will believe in just about anything," Qayum says softly.

"Is that what you tell yourself now? Your entire world was centered around your faith. I could visit the same sacred sites alone and never experience the same spiritual resonance that I felt with you.

What was fascinating about your belief was that you could find God anywhere and in any form. I've known a lot of religious people, but none who could perform namaz in the mosque, shashtang namaskar to Balaji, and kneel at the altar with equal devotion!

Everyone in school knew of your love for God in all forms. Observing your usual hyperactive, high-energy self transform into absolute stillness in prayer was extraordinary. The vibrations and energy around you were inspiring."

"BK, I think your memory exaggerates just a touch," Qayum says, teasing her friend and trying to lighten her mood. It has the opposite effect on Bhakti. Crestfallen, she asks, "You do not remember any of it?"

"No, It's just that I have not thought about it for a long time." Qayum says, and then, as the memories flood her mind, she continues, "I do remember feeling that absolute stillness deep inside me. I felt whole; everything was perfect, as if nothing else needed to happen. A comforting assurance surrounded me, and I was convinced that all was well and would continue to be well, no matter what…"

Her tone dulls in melancholy, "I thought there was a grand orchestrator of harmony, and everything would be fine. Until it was not."

Bhakti: "So you no longer feel the presence of God or the love?"

Qayum: "It is complicated. It's more like I have not looked for it out of fear of finding only darkness. Science and modern thinkers have found no evidence of any God. I read that most Nobel Prize winners are atheists. Would these intellectually gifted not have found divine evidence or reason to believe if it existed?

I have avoided going to a mosque, church, or temple for a while. If I must visit, I stay guarded. I am afraid to reach out as there might be nothing. Then, all would be truly lost.

But it's not like I am an atheist, either. I have sensed guidance within when I was totally lost or dejected. When difficult questions confronted me, I felt answers revealing themselves to me. Solutions that I could not have formulated on my own. I sense an unexplainable energy that lights my path when life plunges into darkness."

Bhakti interjects, "OK, but if you do not sense the light, then would you declare that God does not exist? God is not your personal torchlight. God is you! I can't find the words to explain it, but I can't imagine being angry with my Krishna because I expect nothing from him. The love I feel fills all the voids in my life. What more could I possibly ask for?"

Bhakti pauses to make eye contact with Qayum, who appears mesmerized by her words, so she goes on, "You know, when I moved to Kenya, leaving my friends, my family, and my home behind in Bombay, I never felt lonely because Krishna's love was in my heart. I perform puja that you might consider illogical. I pray to the statue of Krishna, but that statue is the symbol of divinity because I instill it with the divinity inside me.

Without my own spiritual projection, it is just stone or brass. I know God is not in that statue, but for a moment, I pretend so I can express and experience unattached, limitless love. And, I do not need science to provide proof of my God's existence that I feel so deeply."

Inspired by Bhakti's unbashful admittance of faith, words flow through Qayum as the thought is still forming, "I can now see clearly what happened all those years ago. All the devotion I felt disappeared when I tried to cash it in. I expected my omnipotent holiness would stop the riots, and when She did nothing for the innocent suffering, I felt betrayed and angry. The moment my faith turned transactional, it was lost. I was then left with a void."

Bhakti pats Qayum's arm, "You do not have to feel the void. You said it yourself: there have been times when you have still felt a presence. You can start there. Just start by looking within yourself."

Qayum is hooked on her own train of thought, and she repeats herself, needing to hear it again, "The part I see clearly is that I tried to have a transactional relationship with Allah, and that is where everything fell apart. I get that the divinity is not my personal vending machine, and my faith cannot be based on the condition that my worldly requirements are met."

"Beyond that," she admits, "I do not know how to start reconciling faith. When I felt faith as a child, my mind was simpler. I felt love that I can neither explain now nor do I know how to rekindle.

Now, I have frameworks for reasoning and analysis. I do not know how to fit the love for divinity in any of it. It is not anything like any of the other relationships in my life."

Bhakti: "Well, if you are looking for logic and reasoning, you can start with the most fundamental concept, which is to see that God is not apart from you. You and God are one and the same."

Qayum looks perplexed, so Bhakti continues explaining with her own life example, "You know, when I was attacked and robbed, thinking that Krishna allowed this to happen or asking his help to change the circumstance would have been absurd! It is because He and I are the same. My love for Him gave me strength as I suffered. It is not that I am a part of Him, or He is a part of me. We are the same - inseparable! Do you understand?"

Qayum can feel the intensity of Bhakti's faith but struggles to rationally process the meaning of her words. So she shakes her head to indicate no. This prompts Bhakti to think of a different way to explain.

She points to her gold chain and says, "This chain is made of gold. Can it exist outside of gold? No. Gold is its essence. The chain is only a manifestation of gold. It is a form that gold has taken. The chain is inseparable from gold.[17]"

Qayum clarifies, "So in your analogy, I am the chain, and God is gold; therefore, I am inseparable from God. I am pure gold!"

Bhakti chuckles at the childish humor. Before she has a chance to respond, Qayum continues, "But I am powerless, a limited being and the divinity is infinite; how can divinity and I be the same?"

---

[17] Analogy inspired by Swami Sarvapriyananda's Vedanta Talks.

Bhakti responds, "If you're asked what is gold? You cannot say, 'Gold is this chain.' The chain is just one of its forms. You cannot try to define gold by its form or function. It could take the form of other jewelry, a gold bar, or anything else. Do you understand?"

Qayum hesitates, "The universe is the manifestation of God, and the various objects are its forms. So, I am all of God in one form. If that is true, then why do I feel helpless to control my life? Why am I burdened by emotions like sadness, loss or plagued by physical aches?"

Bhakti is patient and mumbles, "I see where you are stuck." Then, composing her thoughts, she begins, "Who is sad? Where are the aches? Who is lost and helpless?

You need to start with understanding who is the real you. The aches are most likely in the body, the sad and happy feelings are the state of your mind, and the loss of control and helplessness is the assessment of your intellect. Are you your mind, body, intellect, or something beyond that? What are you? You will need to start there."

Upon hearing these words, Qayum feels a shiver run through her as if an intense emotion is surging from within. She shares with Bhakti the introspection she has undertaken in recent days. "Just last evening, I had a revelation about the need to detach from my ego and the sense of entitlement to the results of actions performed by this body, mind, and intellect. Qayum goes on to convey her understanding of the transience of her own existence. In that moment, worldly successes and failures seemed insignificant.

"Yet I don't know how to sustain that feeling without anchoring my identity. When I say 'I,' I mean my ego, body, or mind. If I'm not the body, mind, and intellect, what am I? That's precisely where I landed before meeting you," Qayum admits. "

Bhakti perks up and playfully mimics the treasure hunt games they played as kids, "Hotter and hotter! The treasure may be buried just beneath you."

Then, with a somber reflection continues, "The realization of one's identity and the path leading to it is something we each must find alone. For me, that route was through devotion to Krishna. You will discover your own way." Brightening again, she concludes, "The very fact you're seeking and have made strides in detaching from your physical self and ego signifies you have long embarked on this expedition to self-discovery!"

The friends talk late into the night - Bhakti's Baltic cruise with Mihir's family and their planned excursions in Scandinavian countries. In turn, Qayum shares her own travel plans. The conversation then veers to mutual school friends and who is doing what. At some point, neither remembers exactly when words are surrendered to sleep.

Part 3: The Awakened

The frogs in tropical countries hibernate for several months, staying submerged in muddy waters. When, at last, the skies fill with ominous monsoon clouds, the frogs awaken and preach the harsh truth.[18]

---

[18] Inspired by Swami Chinmayananda's commentary on Mandukya Upanishad with Gaudapada's Karika.

Chapter 10: Catching Up

After landing at Copenhagen Airport, Bhakti and Qayum make their way through immigration, head to the luggage carousel, and grab the bags that seem to be on a joyride for a while, waiting for them.

Scanning the busy pick-up area, Qayum spots a familiar face beaming ear-to-ear. It is Vatsal! Overcome with emotion, she drops her bags and rushes into his arms. They embrace, cherishing their reunion after nearly eight days.

Bhakti hangs back politely, allowing them a moment. When Qayum waves her over, she approaches warmly.

"Vatsal, meet my dear childhood friend, Bhakti," Qayum says. Vatsal smiles, "Wonderful to meet you! I've heard so many stories from Qayum's school days."

Bhakti responds graciously, "Likewise! Your wife has spoken very fondly of you."

After the brief introductions, Bhakti explains she has booked a ride to the port as her cruise departs that evening. She glances at her watch, noting the time with a sigh. Gathering her bags, she bids them a warm goodbye. With tight hugs and promises to meet again soon, Qayum bids her friend farewell. Bhakti is returning back from the cruise on the day of the award ceremony - next Sunday. She has some family event in the evening, so she promises Qayum coffee that Sunday morning.

Qayum watches as Bhakti's car disappears down the street while thanking fate's delightful plot twists that brought them together. An awe arises for the invisible strands of affinity that kept their kindred spirits tethered across time and diversity of experience. Vatsal guides her to their waiting taxi.

During the ride to their hotel, Qayum and Vatsal catch up on all that had transpired during their time apart. She shares highlights from the book tour and the creative solution to the overselling problem they had faced. Vatsal tells her about the productive meetings and client dinners in Chicago and New York.

Throughout their exchanges, Vatsal studies his wife. Something about her seems lighter, maybe brighter than before. Qayum appears more present, attentive to each word he utters. It was as if a weight had been lifted from her spirit.

They soon arrive at Hotel D'Angleterre, where Vatsal has booked a suite overlooking the picturesque Kongens Nytorv square. After the long journeys, they opt for a relaxed evening in. Following quick showers, they change into cozy sweats and order room service.

Over steaming bowls of traditional Danish meatballs with buttered potatoes, Qayum animatedly recounts her revelations from the soul-stirring road trip along the California coast. With great detail, she describes how the long, tranquil drives along the breathtaking coastline had been therapeutic. Contemplating radiant sunsets that painted the sky in dazzling hues helped her internalize the impermanence intrinsic to all phenomena. Through this, she realized that lasting happiness requires being an impartial observer, detached from fleeting experiences.

She confesses her ego's appetite for high performance and external validation. The only way to overcome this need, in her perspective, is the dissolution of the ego. This can be done through internalizing that her actions are not fully her own individual doing but rather a play orchestrated by nature's will.

"I am not sure I fully grasp the role of ego, and why would it bring sorrow?" asks Vatsal, looking thoughtful.

Qayum recounts how her heartache had stemmed from a wounded ego entangled with her professional status and other's perceptions. She discovered her sense of entitlement to praises and rewards. When they did not show up, it fueled resentment.

Her actions, even when praiseworthy, were not her own. Expanding on this idea, she clarified further with specifics of the role nature played in creating both the need for action and the body, mind, and intellect's abilities to perform the action. The ego deserved no credit at all.

After Qayum finishes her perspective, Vatsal sits quietly for a moment, taking in her words. "Ahaa," he then exclaims, "So if you are saying nature is responsible for both the need and execution of actions and ego deserves no credit, then are you implying there is no free will?"

Vatsal's question fills Qayum's head with multiple competing thoughts all at once that she tries to frame into a coherent response. Her brows furrow as she carefully considers the complex issue. Studying Qayum's face, Vatsal adds more context to his question, "I was reading an article by a neurobiologist that says there is no free will as every behavior can be attributed to some neuron in our brain and the environment that conditions us.

He used examples of the color of clothes in our wardrobe to someone pulling a trigger. His conclusion is that every decision we make comes down to genetics and conditioning determining our behavior, and thus, free will does not exist. This controversial view even goes as far as saying we should not have any moral judgment as people are mere biochemical puppets!

Do you agree?"

"Yes, and absolutely not!" Qayum says, laughing. "A while back, I read a paper by Dr. Arindam Chakrabarti on free will and freedom in Indian Philosophies, where he summarizes views from Upanishads, Mahabharata, Samkhya-yoga, Jainism, and Buddhism.

It was intriguing to see how Dr. Chakrabarti skillfully captures the contradictions in every single scripture that describes both the presence of free will (kṛti) or volition (prayatna) and absolute determinism by natural causal laws (niyati).

In the paper, there is a noteworthy story in the 13th chapter of Mahabharata that captures the moral judgment conundrum beautifully through a debate between Gautami, a pious woman whose son is killed by a snake bite, the hunter who wants her permission to kill the snake as a punishment for its deeds and the snake who claims no responsibility.

The hunter wants Gautami to exact retribution. Gautami sees no point in killing the snake as it would not bring back her son or reduce her longing for her lost child. The snake claims it has no free will, it is not independent, and it was not out of spite but propelled by 'death' it bit the son.

It calls upon death or *Mrityu* to plead for his case. *Mrityu* says that it was guided by *Kaala* or time when it sent the snake to bite the child. The all-devouring time creates and destroys everything. However, *Kaala* says that it was the child's *karma* from the past that resulted in his death.

Dr Chakrabarti notes, 'Any rationally reflective person should feel the tussle between destiny and free will, two forces locking horns within the human person like two embattled mountain goats. But what is ordinarily taken to be destiny is just another name for one's own past actions, while free will is effective in one's own present and future actions.'"

Qayum pauses, reflecting on her own perspective. "I personally struggle with the concept of past life karma as it feels like a copout for anything that cannot be explained and is out of our control. I can still call it destiny."

She continues, "Gautami's story highlights destiny's role. While, a wise bird in a previous chapter tells the king that noble ones take the initiative and only the incompetent worship destiny! So are the scriptures saying there is free will, or that everything is predestined? I believe they suggest that the contradictions can co-exist within their boundaries."

Vatsal nods in agreement and adds, "Sure, it is true. We are given a body, mind, and intellect which is pre-configured with capabilities and preferences. These aspects are beyond our control, as are the circumstances of our lives, including the conditioning we receive during our upbringing.

However, it is up to us to be aware of our behavior shaped by conditioning, and we can take action to reshape it within our limited capacities. We are also responsible for our actions or inactions even if the outcomes are not in our control."

"Yeah," says Qayum, "I think the confusion on free will vs. deterministic destiny arises only when you are focused on the results. For instance, the people for whom fate has decided that they could not run because their legs were amputated are still using their power to choose to participate in races using their hands and instruments. The reverse is also true; someone may have the genes to be an olympian, and they may put in all the work.

However, certain circumstances might block them from winning. The result is never in our control, but should that make us give up our ability to take action and just surrender to destiny?"

Vatsal laughs, "I know you never will! However, neuroscientists may argue that you have some genetic advantages. For example, a certain variant of the dopamine D2 receptors makes it easier to resist temptations. Some studies have found that greater white matter mass in the prefrontal cortex helps with self-control.

There is some other evidence suggesting that extra gray matter volume in the amygdala that processes emotions impacts willpower. All of these scientific discoveries tying willpower to genetics and brain structure suggest that having 'free will' is pre-destined! What do you say to that?"

"Umm.. very interesting! I am not entirely sure how to respond. I can only know what is possible to be done with the instruments I have. That is my mind-body-intellect!

And it has not been easy for me to overcome temptations. I have been practicing my metaphorical dance routine, patiently directing the impulsive elephant, which represents my primal urges that are a combined result of nature and nurture.

You know that I have had to observe my instincts and collect a series of tools over decades to direct the body-mind's actions - molding new habits to enable automation, tempering the intensity of built-in likes and dislikes, and maintaining perspectives through life's dualities by visualizing the opposite."

Vatsal, very familiar with this metaphor and Qayum's passion for self-mastery, lets out an amused chuckle with "Nach meri jaan hoke magan tu,[19]" as he gets up to grab the bottle of wine to refill their glasses.

Acknowledging Vatsal's playful reaction, Qayum giggles, "I guess you can rewrite the destiny of free will if you really want to. It takes work and time. For me, the motivation is fairly simple - the body-mind-intellect are the instruments I embody. They are complex and miraculous, and I must be

---

[19] A song from an Indian movie that roughly translates to - Dance, my dear, and lose yourself in the dance.

capable of tending to them for as long as I continue to utilize them. I feel a sense of responsibility for their well-being."

Then, she delves deeper into her insights and admits that mastering physical senses and actions is only a preliminary step. Now, she knows that only by relinquishing her attachment to outcomes and dedicating herself fully to the task at hand would she find lasting peace.

Vividly recalling the rhythmic crash of waves seen from her hotel room in Half Moon Bay, she describes how she had been transported into a state of heightened awareness with a sense of connectedness to all beings. As the salty breeze cooled her skin, baking in the warm sun, she could clearly see the different waves of the ocean water rush to the shore only to be merged back into the ocean. The waves literally resembled all the people at work. In that moment, victory, loss, social status, and power seemed so unimportant. The only thing that was obvious was that each wave would soon crash onto the shore and be merged into the water again.

Qayum acknowledges how the realization of the transiency and brevity of our existence made the wounds of the past feel irrelevant. She felt liberated. Yet an enduring peace required finding an unshakable anchor for her identity. She describes being left with the puzzle - if not the mind-body-intellect or even ego - then what was the essence of her being?

Vatsal listens intently, asking several clarifying questions and digging into details. They had discussed the underlying philosophies in the past; however, listening to Qayum's introspection and revelations made the abstract seem more practical.

After their satisfying dinner, they step out onto the balcony with glasses of velvety Merlot. The cool night breeze gently tousles Qayum's hair as she leans her head on Vatsal's shoulder. Infatuated with the dazzling city lights, they sit in tranquil silence, simply soaking up each other's presence and thinking about their enriching exchange.

Qayum is amazed by how readily Vatsal can grasp the complexities of her experience. He is impressed by her perseverance and mesmerized by her vivid articulation.

She breaks the silence to describe the unexpected meeting with her long-lost friend Bhakti and how Bhakti's arranged marriage had taken her to Kenya, her unbelievable stories from the vastly different life path.

Despite the gap of several decades and the divergent directions their lives had taken, their bond instantly reappeared as if it was always there. It almost seemed that Bhakti had appeared out of nowhere only to remind Qayum of who she used to be and reflect on notions of faith and identity.

Bhakti expressed conviction that they were all essentially divine beings temporarily masked in earthly forms. While Qayum admired Bhakti's unfaltering spiritual devotion, she could not profess the same convictions.

Their conversation sparked contemplation. Vatsal had always been curious about faith, yet found it did not align with his logical reasoning and criteria for acceptance. Qayum concludes her narration, landing at the curious intersection where her quest for her identity had been reignited twice on the same day!

As it nears midnight, Vatsal lightly brushes a wisp of hair from Qayum's cheek, tucking it behind her ear and asking, "Shall we turn in? We should try to make the most of tomorrow's sightseeing opportunity." Nodding, she follows him back inside their suite.

They perform their nightly rituals side-by-side - brushing, changing, and applying lotion. Slipping under the silky sheets, Qayum rests her head on Vatsal's chest. His steady heartbeat and warmth are comforting. Within moments, they drift into a blissful sleep.

Chapter 11: What Am I?

Meanwhile, in the other realm beyond time and space, the supernatural forces mull over how best to guide the detached seekers of truth. Amidst snow-capped mountains, bright wildflowers bloom in vibrant patterns, bouncing off the sun's radiance. The hues of violet, gold, and cerulean unfold fractal patterns as they dance in the gentle zephyrs that carry their fragrance.

The paths to liberation begin by contemplating the 'Self' or 'Divinity.' However, tenacious faith in the divine is rare in modern times, while belief in one's own existence remains universally accepted. Thus, focusing on the 'Self' may resonate most with seekers today.

This irrefutable truth of one's being was demonstrated by René Descartes, the 17th-century French philosopher and mathematician, In an era when many thinkers relied upon assumptions Descartes considered false, he sought to establish knowledge grounded in certainty, truths so undoubtable they could withstand even the most skeptical scrutiny. To unravel what could be known beyond any doubt, he employed a method of radical skepticism, rejecting any idea that could be called into question. He began by doubting the reliability of all his beliefs, including his very perceptions, memories, and even the existence of the external world.

Through this systematic demolition of all that could be uncertain, he discovered one fact that remained indubitable - that he was able to think and, therefore, must exist on some level. After all, even if he was merely being deceived by an illusory world, there must be an "I" to be deceived. This unshakeable truth led to Descartes' famous declaration, "Cogito ergo sum" - "I think, therefore I am." With this singular realization, Descartes established a firm philosophical grounding for knowing the existence of 'Self' with certainty.

Armed with this context, we can tune into Sakshi's broadcast: "Since you can be certain of your own existence as a thinking-feeling entity, you can start your inner journey there. Contemplate your identity through a two-step process. First, understand what you are not on the most fundamental level. This helps eliminate misperceptions. Then, you can gain insight into who you truly are at your core. What you are thinking of as your own self is not the real you."

Expanding on Sakshi's guidance, Maya adds, "In daily life, we often refer to our 'I' as our body when hungry, our mind when happy, or our intellect when comprehending information. Yet beneath all these changing states, there exists something more fundamental that is aware of each of these varied experiences. The ancient scriptures name this underlying essence as the 'Atman' or the 'Self—the substrate of our being that remains unchanged behind the shifting veil of all our individual states, moods, and expressions."

Though ultimately impossible to fully describe, the 'Self' is said to be unseen, unheard, unfelt through any physical sense. It has no definable attributes that could be captured through language or conceptualized through examples. This 'Self' has no limitations or properties that could be ascribed to a finite being. There was never a time when the 'Self' was born or came into existence, nor will there be a time when it ceases to exist. While our bodies and minds are ever-changing, the 'Self' is the only unchanging reality[20], the substratum on which the grand illusion of the universe dances.

The truth-seeker can discern the unreal and face it with strength. What is real requires no enduring[21]

Adding to the discourse, Prakruti notes, "Throughout history, there have been rare beings who awakened to this deeper truth of their own 'Self' and manifested profound wisdom. Some of these enlightened sages chose to construct 'ladders' to guide others on the spiritual path—the philosophical scriptures and texts. They aimed to share timeless methods for seekers to realize their own true 'Self.'"

---

[20] Bhagwad Gita Verses 2:13-2:14. See Appendix
[21] Bhagwad Gita Verses 2:15-2:16. See Appendix

The 'ladders' Prakruti refers to are the old scriptures written by people who found liberation in their true identity. These ancient texts equate the individual 'Self' with the absolute reality or divine essence, which is given names like Brahman in the Upanishads. Here are some examples with the names of the Upanishads for reference:

Aham Brahmasmi: I am Brahman (Brihadaranyaka)
Ayam Atma Brahma: This Self is Brahman (Mandukya)
Prajnanam Brahma: Consciousness is Brahman (Aitareya)
So'ham: I am That (Isha)

The 'Atman,' 'Brahman,' and 'Sakshi' point to a fundamental force interweaving existence. Across eras and continents, independent traditions and cultures worldwide have recognized this spiritual substratum as the primordial ground of being:[22]

In America, the Lakota referred to it as Wakan-tanka, translated as the 'Great Spirit' or 'Great Mystery'

The Amazonian Ufaina call it Fufaka, a vital force present in all living things.

Over in Japan, the Ainu termed it Ramut, translating to "spirit energy."

---

[22] Taylor, S. (2020), An Introduction To Panspiritism. See references for details

Imunu, meaning "universal soul," is what the indigenous peoples of New Guinea decided to call this essence.

This spiritual energy differs from the common conception of a deity demanding worship and overseeing worldly affairs. Rather, it is envisioned more as an omnipresent, cosmic power—infinite, eternal, impartial, beyond limitations like gender or personality traits. The Brahman envisioned by the ancient Rishis aligns with this notion of an abstract, unifying power as opposed to a personal, anthropomorphic God.

To make such vast, abstract concepts accessible to spiritual seekers, the sage narrators artfully employ dialogues where the aspects of the 'Self' are questioned and unpacked. In this tradition, today, Prakruti represents the queries of the seekers across eons, "Why expend such effort realizing this 'Self' that is formless and abstruse?"

In response, Sakshi explains plainly, "You continue to suffer, perceiving this world falsely as concrete reality when, in truth, it is a kaleidoscopic mirage projected by consciousness. We established previously that what you attribute to ego, body, and mind as personal victories or defeats are enacted entirely by primordial nature.

Freedom from life's melancholy lies in transcending this illusion by realizing your individual beliefs, identities, and perceptions of the external universe are only transient appearances —they do not define your true essence in any way. Once grasped, this truth has the power to liberate one from bondage to mental anxieties and external phenomena."

"But if the ultimate reality or true 'Self' is incomprehensible by the conceptual mind and senses, why not simply remain content in this familiar illusion that constitutes the world I currently know?" Prakruti presses further on behalf for the human seekers.

"Because without access to higher truth, you cannot be truly happy or free," Sakshi elucidates. "Believing yourself fundamentally finite - defined by your body-mind-intellect - perpetuates lack and incompleteness. In the illusion, there is you - the 'Self' and everything else 'Not-Self' or 'Unatman.'

In contrast, properly realizing your own limitless, unchanging nature enables transcending mental traps of ceaselessly chasing pleasures and resisting the unpleasant.

It is Maya's turn, and she decides to leverage the scriptures already known to humanity. She states, "Buddha's lifelong quest led him to a diagnosis pinpointing 'desire is the root cause of all suffering.'

Chandogya Upanishad has a unique poetic perspective: 'That which is infinite is the source of happiness. There is no happiness in the finite. Therefore, one must try to understand what the infinite is.' [23]

Here, the sage Sanatkumāra teaches his student, Nārada, about the nature of happiness using the word "bhūmā" to denote the infinite. He explains there can be no lasting happiness in the finite because it is incomplete and impermanent.

For instance, finite riches demand continual accrual, finite bodily capacities necessitate enhancing skills, and finite beings, irrespective of how much power or influence they have amassed, will always need more.

Associating our sense of self with worldly objects and the limited body-mind-intellect ties us to the finite. The finite can never be satisfied no matter how much one attains. The infinite, by contrast, cannot need anything more.

As the infinite, we are one with everything, and nothing is apart from us. Anyone who realizes this truth is free from the shackles of desire.

Let me tell you the story of the 'Princess of Kashi' that will illustrate this point. In a distant kingdom, a King and Queen were holding festivities that included theatricals. For their

---

[23] Mantra 7.23.1 from Chandogya Upanishad
yo vai bhūmā tatsukhaṃ nālpe sukhamasti bhūmaiva sukhaṃ bhūmā tveva vijijñāsitavya iti bhūmānaṃ bhagavo vijijñāsa iti || 7.23.1 ||

play, they needed a young child to play the 'Princess of Kashi.' The Queen proposed that the prince, who met the age requirement, should take on the role for the performance.

At the end of the play, the Queen, enchanted by the innocent charms of the little prince, commissioned a portrait of him in his princess guise. The year was neatly noted on the painting labeled 'Princess of Kashi.'

Over 15 years later, the boy-turned-man stumbled upon the very same portrait in the dust-laden palace attic. Noting the date on the painting, he saw not a little girl but an exquisite vision of a woman around his own age.

A yearning bloomed within him. He was consumed by a desire for this eternal beauty captured on canvas, and over the ensuing months, his world was shrouded in melancholy.

At last, the baffled King enlisted his wise minister. Seeking to understand what was causing the prince distress, the minister confronts the prince. The amusing truth is revealed to both – the brooding prince had simply fallen for his own younger self portrayed years ago!

When the prince learned that the portrait was his own, all his desires for the 'Princess of Kashi' vanished."

Gleefully, Maya concludes her story with, "We can only desire that which is separate from us."

Prakruti now poses the ultimate question, "How can the spiritual seeker grasp their true essence in a tangible way?"

Sakshi responds, "The sages employ skillful means through tailored metaphors, stories, and teachings intended to resonate with seekers according to their culture and paradigm. These tools serve as pointers toward the truth, gradually refining the seeker's understanding."

To illustrate such practices, Sakshi taps into the mindstream of Qayum, a modern spiritual aspirant seeking self-realization. In Qayum's dream state, she envisions herself as a colossal silver screen in a cinema hall, projecting a movie. She has no control over which movies get chosen to be projected on her - whether comedies, tragedies, emotional dramas, action films, or mysteries.

As the projector whirs to life, she feels the first show materialize within her consciousness. The opening credits roll as the theater fills with eager moviegoers clutching popcorn and drinks. Excitement fills the air.

A family comedy unfolds, the characters bumbling through misadventures. Qayum experiences the audience's laughter arising within her, though as the screen, she is unaffected by the movie that is playing.

The movie transitions into a heart-wrenching tragedy as mournful music swells. Though tears well in the eyes of the audience, Qayum remains unmoved, a dispassionate observer who enables the movies to play out. Next, an action thriller emerges, the audience gripping their seats as suspense unfolds. Yet Qayum, the screen itself possesses no faculty to react.

With each sequence change, Qayum realizes she is the illumination behind every character, every joy, tragedy, fight, and shock. Though the stories come and go, she remains unaltered. When, at last, the final credits roll and the theater empties, no trace remains of the vivid movies that had played minutes before. Qayum stands empty yet fulfilled. No cinematic explosion has scarred her; no beautiful scenery has added to her persona.

A deep voice instructs clearly, "You are the unchanging, eternal reality upon which the grand play of worldly illusions unfolds. You cannot be tainted or enhanced by what is fleeting and unreal."

The setting in Qayum's dream shifts to a room filled with electrical appliances. She hears the hum of the refrigerator and the blinking buzz of the microwave clock. The aroma of toast wafts from the toaster as it pops up golden brown slices. Here, she is the electricity that powers each gadget - toaster, blender, microwave - into its purposeful existence.

She glows as the light bulb, illuminating the room in a warm, yellow glow. She circulates as a fan, creating a cool breeze that flutters papers on the desk. And she warms as a floor heater, sending waves of comforting heat across the room. Qayum feels herself coursing as surging currents through the wires unencumbered by the limiting shells of the appliances. She flows ceaselessly her essence never depleting no matter how many devices she energizes. She is the life force awakening each contraption, yet nothing can contain her.

The devices—the lamp, the fan, and the heater—are mere vessels enabled by her energy. Their unique forms and functions cannot limit or change her inherent boundless nature. Also, she cannot make the appliance perform functions it does not already possess. The whispering voice concludes, "You are the deathless, persistent awareness observing and sustaining each passing experience of the body and mind. You transcend the physical limitations of the mind-body-intellect you incarnate."

There is a story of a young boy around 8 years old who was wandering near the River Narmada, seeking a Guru. He encountered a seer who asked him, "Who are you?" In response, the boy composed a song called Nirvana Shatakam[24] to explain what he is and what he is not:

---

[24] In Sanskrit nir means no and vana means form or vibration sounds associated with existence. So, Nirvana means formless or soundless. Shata means six so Shatakam is six stanzas.

The little boy was Adi Shankaracharya, ofcourse!

'Six Stanzas of the Formless

I am not the mind, intellect, ego, or reflected awareness;
Not the senses that hear, smell, taste, or see;
Not space, earth, fire, or wind;
I am the eternal form of consciousness-bliss. I am Shiva!

I am neither the breath nor its five components of air,
Not the seven minerals nor the five sheaths of the body,
Not organs of speech, motion, procreation, or excretion;
I am the eternal form of consciousness-bliss. I am Shiva!

I have no malice or desire nor greed and attachment;
I have no sense of possession nor preoccupation with status
or appearance;
I am not bound by the pursuits of duty, acquisition,
consumption, or liberation.
I am the eternal form of consciousness-bliss. I am Shiva!

I am not virtue or sin, nor am I joy or sorrow;
I am not the sacred utterances, sites, scriptures, or rituals;
I am not the act of devouring, the consumed or consumer;
I am the eternal form of consciousness-bliss. I am Shiva!

I do not doubt death and do differentiate based on birth.
I am not a father or mother, nor was I born,
I have no relations, no friends, no teacher, no disciples,
I am the eternal form of consciousness-bliss. I am Shiva!

I am changeless and formless,
I rule over and permeate all the senses (in the body-mind),
I seek neither attachment, nor detachment, nor liberation,
I am the eternal form of consciousness-bliss. I am Shiva!'

Recalling the story and song, Prakruti resumes her line of philosophical questioning, digging deeper into the discourse on the 'Self': "You speak of a seeker looking for one's true nature beyond limitations, but if the seeker is the unchanging, eternal, unborn, and undying, 'Self' what are they searching? What is the liberation from?"

Sakshi nods approvingly, "You raise an insightful query. The enlightened know there is truly nothing to attain or realize, for the 'Self' is ever-perfect and unconditioned by experiences. However, most souls remain obscured by the veil of illusion, identifying with their limited body-minds. Realization is the unraveling of this false identification, the dropping of limiting attributes to see one's true nature."

Maya adds, "While the absolute truth is that there is nothing to attain, most souls require a process of awakening to the truth. These illumined dreams and metaphors spark insights that gradually thin the veils of delusion. When the veils fully dissolve, the ever-present truth shines forth effortlessly."

Chapter 12: It's a Dream

The morning rays of golden light streaming through sheer curtains gently rouse them awake. Sensing Vatsal's presence, Qayum suddenly remembers the vivid dreams from the previous night. She sits up in bed, staring at the beams of light pouring in and revealing the millions of dancing particles. It feels like she is dreaming right now.

Vatsal whispers, "Good morning, sleepy head, did you sleep well?"

"Yeah, like a log, and you?" responds Qayum, still unsure if she is really awake.

"I feel well rested," Vatsal responds, and noticing that Qayum is lost in thoughts, adds, "Tell me about your dream."

"I need a run first. Wanna come?"

"Only if we can walk and talk," Vatsal says, stretching his arms overhead. He gives Qayum a fond kiss before heading in to change into his running clothes and shoes.

Soon after, they make their way outside into the brisk Copenhagen morning. The breeze is just right, and the sun is up but still below the buildings as they set off from their hotel near Kongens Nytorv Square. The historic architecture creates a quaint scenery as Qayum considers narrating her mystical dreams from the night before.

She struggles to put her visions into words. "I can't seem to find the words to accurately describe the experience," she says. "It felt so authentically real, just like you can feel these cobblestones beneath your feet right now. But trying to explain it makes it sound crazy. It most definitely explained what I am."

With an apparent uncertainty, she continues, "In the dream, it was as if everything that appears real, like places, people, things, etc., did not truly exist. I remember vividly seeing the world - I mean people, places, things - as just a projection - for lack of a better word.

I was like the illumination by which all people, places, and things, including my own body-mind persona, were made possible. I could not see the real me, so I cannot be sure, but I felt like I was an ever-present entity, like the screen enabling a movie to be projected in a theater."

As they round the corner, leaving the manicured gardens of the square, Qayum explains how past events played out on her screen of awareness like a movie. "There were funny moments that made the audience laugh hysterically. I could see my persona interacting with other characters in the scenes. But the real me simply remained the backdrop, allowing it all to unfold without any reaction.

I was merely an observer, unaffected by the joys and sorrows unfolding before me. I possessed no body or mind to feel joy or pain. And with no intellect, I could not judge whether the experiences were good or bad. I was free, just a silent witness!"

They walk briskly along the cobblestone lanes, passing the imposing columns of the prominent Marble Church that they both take in. With sunshine warming their shoulders, Qayum continues, "Then there were times when I was the electricity powering appliances, unable to control their functions. I could only enable what each device was meant to do, bound by its physical form. Umm.. like I could not get the fan to provide warmth!"

Vatsal, who has been patient and curious as Qayum searched for the right words, now bursts in with a witty remark, "Like I cannot get this body to fly up and get an ariel view of this beautiful city,"

"Yes!" giggles Qayum, "And more importantly it gives me a new perspective with regards to people who I find annoying or intolerable. This new outlook is also very liberating, as I now see their behavior as just a function of their body-mind machinery, which does not really exist outside of my perception."

Up ahead, the striking spirals of the modern corner building come into view. As they walk in silence for some time, her revelations play over in his mind - consciousness a projection screen or electric currents animating gadgets. He considers them very effective metaphors, signaling the dawning of awareness. The serenity in her demeanor conveys the transformation which is well on its way.

Qayum describes the resonant voice, concluding she is the ceaseless awareness behind each passing thought and sensation. With some awkwardness, she admits, "The thing is...right now, I still feel like I am in that same dream. It's as if everything around me only exists because my senses and mind can construct the knowledge of its existence.

I am aware that the body is walking based on the decisions of the mind or intellect. I feel separated from the world and even my own body. Even as I say 'I,' my point of reference has shifted."

By now, they have reached the pleasant waterside promenade of Langelinie. Soft ripples lap against the sides of yachts and small pleasure boats moored at the docks. Out in the distance, the Kastellet star fort glimmers in the morning sun.

Vatsal puts his arms around Qayum as they enjoy the unreal panorama. He wants to agree with Qayum that the beauty around them seems like a dream, knowing well that it is not exactly what she meant. Instead, he softly says, "Have you heard the tale of King Janka?"

Qayum shakes her head, curiosity piqued by the reflective look in Vatsal's eyes. Taking this as his cue for a story, Vatsal begins animatedly describing King Janka's dream adventure.

"One night, King Janka is sleeping in his palace when his security guard rushes in and wakes him, shouting that they are under attack! The king quickly assembles his generals, but despite their heroic efforts, his army is soon overwhelmed by the enemy's sheer numbers. King Janka is captured, bonded, and presented to the enemy king.

King Janak puts up a brave face and prepares to meet death. However, the enemy king decides to spare his life on the condition that Janak never returns to his kingdom. Janka is stripped of his royal attire, given ragged clothes, and dropped at the edge of the kingdom.

Now dressed as a commoner, Janka journeys through the forest to find refuge. He grows desperately hungry and searches for food but finds nothing. At last, he comes to a temple where a wealthy woman is feeding the poor. The starving king joins the long line of beggars, eagerly awaiting the offerings of lentil rice and bread.

When the lady reaches the king, she runs out of bread. The famished king sheds his dignity and spreads out his grimy, cupped palms to collect the lentil and rice.

Just then, a large crow swoops in to steal some of his food. The king loses his balance, and the remaining morsels fall into the dirt.

Utterly distraught, the humiliated king collapses in despair with no will to go on. As he hits the ground, he lets out a loud cry."

As she envisions King Janka's despair, Qayum is struck by how fortune's wheel can spin in a moment, turning even kings into paupers.

Vatsal continues, "To his shock, the cry awakens King Janka in his royal chamber. Catching his breath, he realizes it was just a vivid dream. At first, he is relieved."

"Oh! He was dreaming!?" Qayum exclaims, feeling better on behalf of the king

Vatsal nods. "Yes, but soon, a troubling thought takes hold - how can he be certain this luxurious palace and his kingship are not also part of an elaborate dream? Perhaps his true reality is that of the penniless, desperate beggar.

Hearing his earlier scream, the guard rushes in, and the king asks, 'Yeh sach ya woh sach?' [Is this real, or was that real?]. Perplexed, the guard rushes to find the queen. When the queen arrives, the king asks the same question.

The royal physician is called, and then the advisors and ministers are summoned. Nobody is able to answer the king's question or figure out what is wrong with him."

Vatsal's narration against Copenhagen's baroque architecture and pastel cafés accentuates the imagery.

As they circle back towards their hotel, Vatsal concludes, "The search for the answer goes on until a sage named Ashtavakra comes to his court and explains, 'Na yeh sach, na woh sach, keval tu hi sach!' This translates to neither this is real, nor that was real. You alone are real!"

Qayum is speechless as the parable so closely resembles her own experience. She, too, had floated through dreams where reality felt fluid, leaving her questioning what was real. Like King Janka, her perspective has irrevocably shifted.

Chapter 13: Croaking Clarity

Back in their hotel room, Qayum showers while Vatsal orders breakfast from room service.

Re-energized after washing off her run, Qayum joins Vatsal on the balcony overlooking the bustling city streets below.

As they eat freshly baked bread with jams, yogurt, muesli, and swirling cups of coffee, Qayum and Vatsal plan out their Copenhagen sightseeing for the next few days.

Still processing the surreal dreams and philosophic tale, Qayum remains in a tranquil, meditative state. Her senses feel heightened, attuned to the beauty surrounding her.

Later that day, they wander through the iconic rainbow-hued buildings of Nyhavn Canal, and Qayum soaks up the charming scenery.

On the second day, they embark on a train ride to the coastal town of Helsingør. Outside the window, the idyllic Danish countryside rolls by in a blur of bright green fields and quaint villages.

Touring the imposing Kronborg Castle, Qayum admires the ancient battlements jutting dramatically into the steel-grey sea. She is enthralled picturing the aristocratic extravaganzas and scheming ploys that these walls have witnessed through the centuries.

That evening, Vatsal scours the internet, searching for perspectives to better comprehend Qayum's visions. He stumbles upon an English translation of the Mandukya Upanishad and commentaries from the great 8th-century philosopher Gaudapada. The philosopher uses logic and reasoning to explain the cryptic verses that examine the transient and illusionary characteristics of the universe. Vatsal sees parallels to Qayum's experience and continues his research through the various versions of translations.

Over the next two days, they enjoy Copenhagen's gardens and pedal through bustling city squares. At Amalienborg Palace, they watch the changing of the guard, the royal uniforms sparkle with gold braiding. As they pedal across the canal's bridges, Qayum feels herself becoming one with the bike, joyfully gliding through this storybook city.

On the fifth day of their Copenhagen sojourn, Vatsal rises early, eager to share the fruits of his research on the Mandukya Upanishad with Qayum.

He pulls out his tablet and reviews the various translations, carefully selecting the most lucid verses to discuss.

After a brisk morning walk along the canal and relishing a hearty breakfast, Qayum inquires about their plan for the day.

Putting on an air of mystery, Vatsal reveals, "I have a special outing in mind for us today." Intrigued, Qayum readies for the surprise excursion.

Consulting reviews and maps, Vatsal chooses a charming café named "Verdenshjørnet," which aptly translates to "The Corner of the World." Hidden within the jungly Botanical Garden, this cafe is renowned for its secluded nooks surrounded by vibrant flora.

They embark on a short bus ride through Copenhagen's gorgeous cobbled streets. Verdenshjørnet exudes an old-world appeal with its ivy-cloaked exterior and weathered wooden tables. The ambiance harmoniously blends rustic and modern elements, with soft jazz melodies enveloping the space.

Claiming a plush sofa nook, Qayum settles in, anticipation gleaming in her gaze at Vatsal. With a scientist's glee, he leans forward to share, "I have been doing some research on - if the world is an illusion or dream or in some way unreal, then what is real, and how do we anchor ourselves in reality? There are very straightforward explanations in several Upanishads. I picked Mandukya[25] for us to go through as it

---

[25] See the Appendix for the core 12 Mantras translated using my pick and axe approach of looking at each Sanskrit word ensuring nothing is lost in interpretations.

is the shortest and most potent. It will be perfect for our short time here. What do you say?"

"Sounds great!" responds Qayum eagerly. "Did you say man-doo-kya?"

Vatsal: "Yes! Mandukya means frog in Sanskrit. The frogs hibernate for several months, absorbed in Self like the yogis. When life presents challenges, symbolized by dark rain-filled skies, these frogs let out loud, harsh croaks. Though jarring, their croaking carries a message of truth that provides solace when it is most needed."

Qayum agrees, "How interesting!" then, after a pause adds, "Truth is almost always harsh, but when offered with clarity and compassion can nurture growth."

Vatsal, pleased with his choice of text, continues, "Yes, well said! And there is another important lesson from the frog - just as it pushes back for a leap forward, the ancient texts call upon us to withdraw from worldly attachments to leap into spiritual truth. The Mandukya Upanishad guides us in this leap."

Qayum smiles, amused by his enthusiasm. She takes a sip of her hot tea, sinking back into the velvety sanctuary of the sofa. The murmur of conversations and the occasional clink of cups and saucers create a soothing chorus as Vatsal begins reading his notes, "The first mantra says.."

Qayum jumps in, "Wait, what is the difference between mantra and shloka? Are they interchangeable?"

"No. Mantras are original verses from the ancient Vedic scriptures, including the Upanishads. The Upanishads are philosophical texts contained within the Vedas. The mantras are specific verses from any Vedic scriptures. When recited with the specified intonation, they create vibrations to have a particular effect on the body and mind. Shlokas, by contrast, are longer poetic or devotional verses from later texts like the Bhagavad Gita."

Awestruck, Qayum says, "So cool! You have really researched this!"

With a scholarly demeanor, Vatsal continues, "The first mantra says - Om symbolizes the totality of existence - the past, present, and future, and everything that exists beyond time and dimensions. Atma represents the individual self, which is one with the divine essence, Brahman. This unified self manifests through four states of awareness."

Qayum interrupts, "Oh! So thousands of years ago, they already were thinking of multi-verses and multi-dimensions?"

Vatsal continues enthusiastically, "In fact, the Vedas contain entire sections revealing remarkably advanced scientific knowledge. For example, precise details about human anatomy, surgical procedures, the planets, stars, and even

168

the earth's circumference and axial tilt. It's astounding that ancient seers discerned such truths about the universe and natural world that eluded science for centuries later."

Amused by his wife's uncharacteristic speechlessness, Vatsal chortles as he steers back to the Upanishad. "This unified self manifests through four states of awareness. Waker is the first state of self. It uses limbs and sensory inputs or mouths to engage with the physical world. This state, being the first, attains all that it desires foremost and also becomes the one that knows (Om)."

He looks up thoughtfully and says, "We all know the power of fulfilling desires that our waker state has. We all, at some point, have experienced the ability to make anything we wish for come true."

Qayum supplements, "Yes, though we often struggle to determine what's truly worthwhile to wish for - in the thick of the mind's transitory whims."

Vatsal nods, continuing, "True. Dreamer is the second state of self. It uses the mind's limbs and sensory inputs as mouths to interact with the subtle universe. It is forceful and energetic - as it conjures many different universes with different natural laws and possibilities. This state attains excellence in knowledge with a broad scope and becomes the one that knows (Om)."

He opines, "The dreamer state reveals the extraordinary capacity of our minds to construct entire worlds and planes of reality. Awake, we dismiss dreams as illusions. Yet each night, our dreaming mind effortlessly performs the mystical feat of generating vivid and tangible scenarios, sensations, and beings.

The Upanishad recognizes the sheer power harnessed in this state, able to access truths beyond ordinary waking consciousness. Those who tap into its wellspring can attain cosmic wisdom and creativity. Accounts exist of philosophical or scientific revelations arising in the luminous state between sleep and wakefulness."

Then proceeds to read again, "The third state is the deep sleeper, devoid of desires or dreams. It is an undifferentiated mass of awareness, suspending all possibilities. This source state is the doorway from which all beings originate and terminate. It holds the seed potential for the waker and the dreamer.

Now, the seventh mantra proposes a state of the self that is not conscious of the inner world and not aware of the external world. It is neither conscious nor unconscious. It is only traceable through the unbroken self-awareness of the other three states. Gaudapada calls it Turiya, which means fourth. This state is beyond grasp or description. Ever at peace, this non-dual true essence is what we seek to realize."

Vatsal clarifies how the unbroken continuity of awareness across our changing states points to this eternal, underlying fourth state. When we wake from sleep, we retain the knowledge of having dreamt or experienced dreamless deep sleep. This persistent awareness reveals the existence of Turiya - the silent observer of all states. While the other states are fleeting, Turiya alone is the constant reality.

Scanning through the text, he goes on, "All other states borrow their existence from the fourth as even though existence is fleeting in other states, it is intrinsic to this fourth state - i.e., it never ceases to exist."

Qayum asks, "How do you know transient from intrinsic? I mean, why are the other states changing, and how can you be sure that Turiya is not?"

Vatsal flips through some pages and divulges an explanation that says, "Gaudapada takes an analytical approach to establish the sole reality of the fourth state, Turiya. He examines the difference between permanent, intrinsic attributes versus assumed or borrowed qualities.

This translation uses the example of a potato boiling in the water. We know that the potato is not inherently hot, i.e., it was not hot before it was put in the hot water. The heat in the hot potato was received from the hot water.

Water, by its nature, is also not hot; it has taken its heat from the pot, which derived heat from the fire. The fire is intrinsically hot.

So, the heat from the fire is constant as it persists for as long as the fire exists. The potato's heat is temporary and does not belong to the potato, the water, or the pot. Since it is borrowed, not innate, it is unreal.

Similarly, the universes of waking, dreaming, and deep sleep were not always in existence. These realms manifest and eventually dissolve. Existence, therefore, is not inherent to them. They are impermanent and, thereby, illusory.

Their existence is borrowed from Turiya - the state that is real and pure bliss. It is the state that never ceases to exist."

Contemplating deeply, Qayum verbalizes an imposing thought, "I do not know how to grasp this fourth state - which is precisely what I need to comprehend. The other three states I can experience, but not the fourth state - Turiya!"

"Right." says Vatsal, switching to a different text, he continues, "The commentators use various metaphors to help with the understanding of this fourth state. One such metaphor looks at clay pots, I suppose given the time period of the texts, clay pots were very readily available."

Qayum: "Well, they are pretty common at all pre-historic excavation sites across the globe."

Vatsal nods and reads on, "The clay pots may have different forms and functions like the three states of self we experience, and yet clay is what makes them possible. In this analogy, clay is the Turiya.

If you take away the clay, then there are no clay pots. Turiya makes everything else possible. Only clay has an intrinsic existence, while the pots are temporary names and forms. Like, you can break a clay pot and make a clay pan, and the pan will serve a different purpose than the pot, but their essence remains unchanged as clay."

Qayum's mind instantly flashes back to her conversation with Bhakti aboard the flight just a week prior. Bhakti had shared that the fundamental truth is that God is not separate from oneself. To illustrate this, Bhakti had pointed to her gold necklace, explaining how the chain relies fully on gold for its existence - the chain cannot exist without gold. Qayum had challenged this - how could a limited being be the same as the infinite divine? Yet despite her persistence, Bhakti held firm.

Now, Vatsal is employing a clay analogy to elucidate Qayum's true identity. Piecing it together, Qayum can grasp what Bhakti meant - her body-mind-intellect is the form-function while her real self is inseparable from divinity. The chain is the form-function of gold.

Qayum is staring out at the gardens as she says out loud, "Like, you can melt the locket to make the ring, which will change its form, and the ring will serve a different purpose than the locket, but their essence remains unchanged as gold."

Vatsal responds with, "Yup! You got it!"

Consumed by this vision, Qayum appears frozen in time. After allowing the concept to fully sink in, she brings herself to the present conversation and asks Vatsal, "If Turiya is our true Self, then why is it that we are not aware of it, and why is it that we do not experience it?"

Vatsal: "Because it does not have a form or function. It is not an object, it is what experiences everything. The only way to grasp this is through reason and logic."

"Here is another metaphor," he says, reviewing his notes before proceeding, "The Swami gives an example of a clear lake that reflects the sky, clouds, birds, and everything else around. If we only rely on what we see, our senses can easily trick us into believing that the lake is the sky. However, we use knowledge and reason to understand that there is water in the lake and not the sky. Similarly, we can use logic to identify the state of awareness present in all other states.

Even as we fully comprehend and accept this reality, we do not stop seeing the sky's reflection in the lake. Similarly, the self-realized person continues to see the world's illusions while knowing the real from the unreal.

The universes referred to are the Sthul (gross - physical/waking), Sukshma (Subtle - mind/dream), and Karana (causal - source state/deep-sleep). Our real Self is where none of the universes exist - just like the sun, sky, and clouds do not exist in the lake. They are mere reflections. This fourth state has no desires, performs no actions, and is not all-knowing. Associating one's identity to this fourth state of self, one finds everlasting satiation and peace," concludes Vatsal.

Qayum sits silently as Vatsal's words resonate deeply. She feels centered in the tranquility of the present moment, watching the grandeur of the unreal around her.

Finally breaking the silence, she says, "This is universe-shattering - I mean literally! It sounds great in the moment. But the next moment, as we get busy living real lives, it will be too easy to forget all of this. How do you stay centered in this real self?"

Vatsal switches documents again and ventures further, "Mantras 8 through 12 provide a helpful tool. Using the language rhythm and tones, you can divide Om, which we defined as Brahma's symbol, into four parts: A, U, M, and silence.

Waker's state is constantly encountered and denoted by the first letter A and the **sound ʌ.**[26]

Dreamer's state illuminates and is denoted by the second letter U and the **sound ʊ**.

Deep-sleeper's state, which is awareness, is denoted by the third letter M and the **sound mmm**.

The fourth state, which is boundless, is represented by the character ॐ and with the sound of silence. This state is beyond transactions, fully content in itself, non-dual, and also the one that knows (Om)

Using silence to signify that fourth state, Turiya, is an ingenious way to demonstrate its presence even in the other sounds. The silence is present in the A, U, and M sounds, just like the single unified essence is present in all other states of our being.

By meditating on this idea while chanting Om, focus on the true Self by observing the silence between and during Om chants."

---

[26] See Cambridge Dictionary at
https://dictionary.cambridge.org/us/help/phonetics.html

After their intense discussion on the Mandukya Upanishad, Qayum and Vatsal decide to break for lunch. As they wait for their food, the conversation shifts to lighter topics. Qayum shares amusing anecdotes from her recent book tour events. The avocado toast with smoked salmon is heavenly. Between savory mouthfuls, they reminisce fondly about the wonderful time they've had so far in Copenhagen.

Qayum drifts back to Mandukya Upanishad, and she mumbles, "How astonishing that these insights were already discovered thousands of years ago and then lost to our modern world."

Then, momentarily, she turns inward to her visions, vividly recalling how people and events seemed to flow like waves arising and dissolving back into a vast ocean.

It is obvious that every singular wave—reflecting a person, object, or persona— lacks independent existence. All worldly manifestations prove fundamentally transient, arising from and subsiding back into a limitless sea of unified consciousness and pure bliss.

With her visions subsiding, worries resurface - without replicable evidence, how can awakening experiences transfer from subjective phenomena to shared understanding? How will science objectively penetrate through the material world to find reality?

As the sun hangs lower in the Copenhagen sky, casting a golden dusk glow through their café window, Vatsal emerges from his own introspection and concludes sagely, "The scriptures are illuminating guides, but the journey ultimately unfolds from within. Self-realization cannot be taught, only caught intuitively through reason, reflection, and experience."

They wrap up the day of intellectual and spiritual stimulation with shots of espresso and step outside the cafe for a stroll. The fresh air and vibrant greenery of the Botanical Gardens provide a refreshing contrast to the day's heavy philosophical discussions.

The gentle breeze is loaded with earthy tones of oaks and sweet lilacs. Reflecting on insights from the Mandukya Upanishad, they both wonder if they will be able to remain established in their core self beyond identification with the body-mind or if their insights will fade in the daily grind of life.

As they walk past blooming flower beds and soaring trees, a tale around spiritual practice comes back to Vatsal that makes him chuckle, "Did I tell you my uncle used to lecture us on the Vedas during our summer holidays? We kids did not understand most of what was being said. But I just remembered this funny anecdote he told us. I think it is apt to us fretting about how to cement these insights. So the story goes like this - after gaining knowledge and lessons from the sage Ashtavakra, King Janaka reaches self-realization and begins meditations to stay steady in his newfound insights.

One day, King Janaka is sitting under the shade of a towering banyan tree peacefully in the lotus position, eyes closed. Hands resting on his knees, Janaka is focusing intently on the mantra: 'Aham Brahmasmi (I am Brahma), Aham Brahmasmi Aham Brahmasmi…'

Suddenly, the tranquility is shattered by a grating voice shouting, 'This is my *danda*! This is my *kamandal*!'"

Looking at Qayum, Vatsal confirms," You know danda is the staff, and kamandal is a small pot that sages carry to hold water?"

After getting an acknowledging nod from Qayum, he continues, "King Janaka's concentration wavers as he opens his eyes and sees the sage Ashtavakra sitting right beside him, loudly chanting with his eyes closed.

Annoyed at the interruption, Janaka sighs deeply and moves a few paces over, settling himself under a nearby mango tree. Closing his eyes once more, he resumes his focused meditation, vocalizing the rousing mantra 'I am Brahma, I am Brahma. But soon, Ashtavakra's shrill voice rings out again, now even closer. "This is my staff! This is my pot!"

Furious, Janaka leaps to his feet. "Enough!" he thunders. Ashtavakra stares back calmly as Janaka continues, "Venerable sage, no one here disputes that staff and pot are yours. Must you insist on disrupting my meditation with this pointless chanting?"

Ashtavakra's eyes twinkle with mischievousness and a grin is waiting to reveal itself as he says lightheartedly, "Then surely, O noble king, no one disputes that your true essence is the eternal force of pure bliss. You are Brahma! Then why do you need to keep repeating it?"

Vatsal and Qayum burst into joyful laughter as they can totally relate to King Janaka's need to hold on to the truth.

Then, just like that, with nothing left to grasp - not the fleeting insight, not even the notion of their true identity - a profound sense of liberation and peace descends.

The best friends, unsaddled, sit together on a bench, fingers intertwined, watching dusk dissolve into darkness.

Chapter 14: The Inaction Trap

Qayum is performing the downward dog when she hears the sheets rustle, turns around, and sees Vatsal is awake and sitting up. He smiles at her sleepily, "You are up early!"

"Yup! Good morning!" she beams, "What's plans?"

Vatsal sits up and says, "I need to catch up on some work stuff for a few hours. I was planning to stay in or head down to the cafe and work. What are you thinking of doing?"

"I am off to meet BK for coffee or brunch!" says Qayum with glimmering joy.

"Oh, she is back from the cruise?"

"Yeah, but they are having some family thing in the evening, so she won't be able to join the award ceremony."

As Qayum reflects on the day ahead, her thoughts drift to the award ceremony that evening. She has been nominated for a prestigious literary prize by the International Board for Children. Between her publisher, Prakashay's work to translate her books, and the gentle advocacy of his Danish contact Anna, it is a monumental success. Qayum knows she should feel elated and honored by the nomination, yet oddly, she feels detached. As if the vibrant spectrum of emotions has mellowed into a harmonious blend.

"Liberation from the intensities of pain is also liberation from all kinds of passionate feelings, including exhilaration," notes a passing thought. Qayum consults her phone for directions and takes a quick five-minute walk to Cafe Europa. It is a charming little cafe ensconced between the pretty buildings washed in Scandinavian shades of sage, mustard, and rose. Stepping inside, she spots Bhakti seated at a cozy window table overlooking the bustling street.

Bhakti's face lights up when she sees Qayum enter. After a warm embrace, they settle into the chairs - which are cool, modern, and minimalistic pieces of art. The waitress takes their order - coffee for Bhakti and tea for Qayum.

"How was the cruise? Tell me everything!" Qayum says eagerly.

Bhakti delves into the details of the week-long Baltic cruise with her husband's extended family. She describes the luxurious ship with multiple restaurants, pools, entertainment venues, and spacious suites. During port calls, they explored medieval towns like Tallinn and ancient castles along the Baltic coast. At night, they enjoyed lively music and dancing on the deck beneath the stars.

"It sounds absolutely magical," sighs Qayum. "I'm so glad you got to create these memories together."

Their drinks arrive, and as Qayum savors the aromatic tea, she shares her impressions of Copenhagen. "I am amazed by how welcoming Copenhagners are and love their laid-back attitude. Being in this city is like being transported in time with its cobblestone streets, picture-perfect canals, and historic architecture. At the same time, there are modern, innovative designs and an eco-conscious spirit. Copenhagen blends old-world charms with modern sensibilities, which served as fertile grounds to explore how the timeless spiritual insights can alleviate my modern-day struggles."

Then she recalls her dream, "After our plane talk, I had this dream that seemed to unearth answers about finding my true identity. I saw myself as the unchanging essence while everything else seemed to be mere projections. It's my own vitality that gives existence to the world around me. I finally get that I am the gold in the chain," she says playfully, pointing at the chain around Bhakti's neck.

Bhakti smiles and gives Qayum's shoulder a squeeze. "You know most people need a lifetime to understand this. For me, it was a path carved through deep devotion to Krishna that took decades. And for you to gain these insights so swiftly through a revelation is wonderful! It shows how intensely you wanted the answers."

Ever since the realization began to bloom within her, Qayum became acutely aware of the world's unreality. Yet she also feels intensely mesmerized by the beauty of nature and human feats reflected in the city. The vibrant canal setting outside the cafe window fills her with admiration.

Even looking at the sky, it feels like she is seeing it for the first time—the light blue glowing sky, little fuzzies of floating clouds. Everything is so beautiful! The world seems like a marvelously crafted virtual realm, and with her elaborate VR gear, she has the priceless privilege of experiencing it fully.

She turns to Bhakti, struggling to put her thoughts into words. "Now that I have found the truth, I want to stay in it. I do not want to go back to living in ignorance - struggling for victories, looking for professional recognition, acquiring and holding on to possessions- fancy clothes, house, car, or trying to be well placed in the social order. I do not need any of those things to be happy. Why should I do anything or own any responsibilities in this grand illusion? Why not stay in this self-realized state forever?"

Bhakti smiles, recollecting the time when she had felt similarly. But, since her realization had come more slowly, she had had the time to adjust to the importance of responsibilities and action.

Qayum avoids eye contact with her friend and bashfully whispers, "I wonder if I can just put on orange robes and travel like a monk with nothing and no-one to call my own. Nothing and no-one can then disrupt this peace. Adrift with no attachments, I could just live gazing inward at the unchanging, ever-fulfilling truth…"

"And just converting oxygen to carbon-dioxide!" Bhakti interjects with a laugh. "No Qay! I know you too well. You were never meant to be a renunciate. I know this realization is new to you, and I understand the allure of avoiding any worldly connections that could possibly obscure your insight. But you know that nothing can take it away!"

Qayum frowns, "I do not agree that it cannot be lost."

Bhakti, with a teasing grin: "Did you see your face in the mirror this morning?"

Qayum is puzzled, "Yes. What's your point?"

Bhakti: "You cannot see your face right now because you are talking to me. But are you sure it is still there, or do you need to check on it?"

Qayum does not respond as she parses through Bhakti's analogy.

Bhakti continues, "You are the eternal awareness - not the mind-body-intellect. Even as you engage in worldly interactions, your true self will always be there. You cannot lose it. You do not have to meditate on it."

These words remind Qayum of Ashtavakra from Vatsal's anecdote, chanting, 'The staff is mine. The pot is mine.'

Seeing Qayum fall silent, Bhakti gently continues, "You agree the role you have in this world is brief while your real

185

self is undying. Now imagine if you were acting in a play and were a bandit, would you act out your part as the best possible bandit, or would you need to keep reminding yourself during your bandit-dialogue delivery that you are Qayum only acting as the bandit?"

Qayum laughs, "That would make for a very poor performance!"

Bhakti nods with a sense of triumph. "Exactly! You must fully immerse yourself in playing each temporary role, just like an actor in a performance. Even as you perform your duties, your true essence remains unchanged." The reunited friends sit in silence for a few minutes, finishing their drinks.

"I get what you are saying," admits Qayum. "I do not need to meditate on my real self, that it will still be there when I immerse into worldly action. But why engage at all? What motivates action?"

Then suddenly lighting up, Bhakti declares, "Qay! You are in luck. The entire cosmos is rooting for you."

"BK, what are you plotting now?" Qayum asks with a slight worry accompanying excitement.

Hurrying out of her chair, Bhakti says, "Let's go, or we will be late. I will explain on the way."

The two brisk walk to a bus station on Gammel Strand and wait. Qayum compliments the brightly colored houses lining the narrow Slotsholmens Canal and the view of the Christiansborg Palace across the canal. Just then, the bus arrives, and the two board it, flashing their City Pass.

"Now, will you tell me where we are going?" asks Qayum curiously.

Bhakti responds with excitement, "Yes! Ok. You will not believe this, but there is a Gita reading by a famous monk at the Hindu Temple, just half an hour away. This monk is from Swami Vivekanand's organization. One of my uncles is his great devotee, and the rest of the family is also there. This famous monk just happened to be in Copenhagen giving a sermon on Gita, exactly on the day you need it. Do you see it is not a coincidence?"

Qayum, confused: "No! Wait! Is there a Hindu temple in Copenhagen? What does Gita have to do with what I am struggling with?"

Bhakti sighs and explains more slowly this time, "It may surprise you that the Bhagwad Gita is a more modern, simplified approach for conveying the intricate philosophies of the Upanishads. Unlike the abstract nature of most Upanishads, it uses a story-telling approach with easier-to-read text.

Here's why this is highly relevant to you: After Krishna lays out the simple truth about our eternal, true nature, Arjuna faces a dilemma similar to yours. Why should he fight in a bloody war when he could give up everything and become an ascetic. Krishna explains the importance of not shirking one's duty in this samsara[27]. Since no one can explain as well as the Lord himself, let's listen to what he has to say."

Qayum understands Bhakti's love for Krishna and feels nervous but also curious. She wonders, "What could Krishna possibly say to change my mind?" Then quietly decides, "Let's find out!"

They arrive after a short walk to a brown, cladded building that looks like everything else around it. The sermon seems to be going on for a while now. The two find a spot on the side towards the front of the stage where the priest is seated.

"He will read the shloka from Gita first and then translate it into English. OK?" Bhakti whispers to Qayum, who nods in response. "Looks like they are just starting Chapter 3, which is perfect timing for us."

The monk is singing in a soothing, deep voice:

shrī bhagavān uvācha
loke 'smin dvi-vidhā niṣhṭhā purā proktā mayānagha

---

[27] Samsara is defined as the cycle of death and rebirth to which life in the material world is bound.

188

jñāna-yogena sāṅkhyānāṁ karma-yogena yoginām | 3.3 |
na karmaṇām anārambhān naiṣhkarmyaṁ puruṣho'śhnute
na cha sannyasanādeva siddhiṁ samadhigachchhati | 3.4 |

The monk looks up from the text and begins in clear fluid English, "In Chapter 2 Krishna explained the importance of knowledge through Sankhya Yoga.[28] So, in Shlokas 1 and 2, Arjuna wants to know that if knowledge is superior to action, then why are you asking me to participate in this heinous war?

To this, Lord Krishna responds that knowledge is the path for those inclined to contemplation, and the path of action is for the yogis. The yogi here refers to the person who selflessly carries out their societal duty and divine role without any attachment or selfish desire for personal gain.

Krishna makes it abundantly clear that one cannot escape their assigned responsibility by abstaining from action and retreating into passive renunciation.

Nor can one gain true perfection in knowledge and realization of the Self simply by renouncing the material

---

[28] Sankhya means numbers, and Yoga means union. The union of numbers represents the union of realities that are present in existence. The union emphasizes a single divinity that is neither created nor destroyed, only manifested as pluralities in the universe.

world physically, while the mind remains untrained and undisciplined."

Bhakti nods along approvingly as she is very familiar with the text, while Qayum is transfixed, mesmerized.

The monk continues, "What you need is the practice of controlling the senses through the mind. Knowledge alone is insufficient. You must practice performing your actions without attachment to the accomplishments. You do the action for the sake of action and do it with perfection!"

The monk takes a sip of water, then looks back down at the text to continue reciting and explaining the selected shlokas. "yajñārthāt karmaṇo 'nyatra loko 'yaṁ karma-bandhanaḥ tad-arthaṁ karma kaunteya mukta-saṅgaḥ samāchara |3.9|

You can perform all actions as if there were a fire sacrifice ritual to avoid attachment to the material world. In ancient times, fire sacrifice rituals were performed by putting offerings in the fire. Since most folks do not perform fire sacrifices anymore, there are other ways to internalize this shloka.

Think of the formless, eternal energy that is the core and cause of the world's existence. You can perform your prescribed duties for the benefit of this divinity. For devotees of Krishna, he explicitly calls you to act not for materialism or personal glory but for his sake. For those of you who are still struggling with devotion to God, you can think of your prescribed duties for the benefit of others - society, Earth, and so on.

Perform every action in a spirit of worship, not for ego gratification."

Taking in a deep breath and closing his eyes, the monk recites the next few verses from memory.

"na hi kaśhchit kṣhaṇam api jātu tiṣhṭhatyakarma-kṛit
kāryate hyavaśhaḥ karma sarvaḥ prakṛiti-jair guṇaiḥ |3.5|
prakṛiteḥ kriyamāṇāni guṇaiḥ karmāṇi sarvaśhaḥ
ahankāra-vimūḍhātmā kartāham iti manyate |3.27|
tattva-vit tu mahā-bāho guṇa-karma-vibhāgayoḥ
guṇā guṇeṣhu vartanta iti matvā na sajjate |3.28|"

He opens his eyes and looks directly at his eager listeners, and continues, "In the fifth shloka, Krishna asserts that no one can refrain from action even for a moment. Every being is helplessly forced into action by nature's laws. We must act to sustain our bodies - to quench thirst and hunger, keep ourselves clean, and so on.

These innate biological needs create an impulse to act that is fundamental and cannot be overcome. No matter how spiritually realized you become, you cannot completely abstain from eating, drinking, sleeping, and other natural necessities required to maintain the body.

191

Now, in Shloka 27 and 28, he pinpoints nature as the cause from which the requirement for action originates, and nature is also the enabler of conducting all activities. Only an ignorant person thinks that 'I did this.' This crucial concept - that our actions arise from Prakriti and we are not the true doers - is repeated several times by Krishna in the Gita. He wants to uproot the fundamental misunderstanding about our role as the accomplisher.

In contrast to the ignorant, egoistic person from Shloka 27, the wise, discerning person knows that the need for all activities originates in the mind and belongs to the world of the mind. Therefore the wise are not attached to success-failures, likes-dislikes, love-hatred.

Equipped with this internal freedom, they can perform the action flawlessly like a graceful athlete single-mindedly focused on the sport rather than victory or defeat.

mayi sarvāṇi karmāṇi sannyasyādhyātma-chetasā
nirāśhīr nirmamo bhūtvā yudhyasva vigata-jvaraḥ | 3.30 |

In the 30th Shloka Krishna compels us to dedicate all actions to him. These actions need to be conducted with a focused mind and without any desire, ego, or sense of ownership. And, without any lethargy."

The monk's gaze locks with Qayum's as if sensing her struggle. He says gently yet firmly, "When faced with intense situations, it is tempting to escape responsibility, renounce all action, and retreat into contemplation. Even the great warrior Arjuna wished to do so in the midst of battle. But for you... most of you, now is not that time

For now, you must accept obligations arising from your innate nature and role. Perform your duties mindfully with an attitude of service rather than to fulfill the desires of your ego or intellect.

Fulfill your duties sincerely because it is the right thing to do. Lift your efforts and your work above egoistic impulses and offer it to the Divine through the fire of sacrifice - this is the core of karma yoga.'"

The monk then looks down at the open Gita sitting on a bookholder in front of him, flips through some pages, and announces. "After lunch, we will explore the differences between action and inaction in Chapter 4."

Qayum is in a state of trance, staring at the monk, oblivious as devotees line up for communal lunch. Bhakti waits patiently before whispering, "What do you think? Want to use your opportunity to perfect detachment?"

"What opportunity?" mumbles Qayum, seemingly emerging from her contemplative stupor.

"Your life as a mother, daughter, wife, sister, friend, techie, author - every role is an opportunity! Do you want to give it all up and live the life of a renunciate?"

"Hmmn.. I do not know. This gave me a lot to digest and think through. But right now, I am so impressed with the clarity and relevance of this ancient wisdom to our modern lives. BK, I cannot thank you enough for bringing me here."

"You're so very welcome." Bhakti smiles warmly. "Shall we have a quick temple lunch before you return to the hotel? You likely want to start preparing for the ceremony tonight, right?"

"Yes!" smiles back Qayum, slowly standing up while stamping her feet as circulation returns in prickly waves.

Part 4: The Absolute

When the mirror of the mind is clean, clear, and so still, then 'That' which cannot be known or seen is always shining forth.

Chapter 15: Equanimity

Vatsal and Qayum walk into the grand ballroom of the National Museum of Denmark, immediately struck by the electric ambiance of excitement and anticipation. The cavernous room is filled to capacity with an eclectic mix of people from all walks of life - renowned authors, publishers in sharp suits, flamboyantly dressed illustrators, bespectacled librarians, and, of course, the young readers accompanied by their proud parents.

The air is abuzz with animated conversations and spurts of children's laughter that echo through the vaulted hall. Qayum feels a sense of kinship with every face in the room, united by a common love for the magical world of children's literature.

As they weave their way through the lively crowd to find their assigned seats, a familiar laugh catches Qayum's attention. She turns around and spots Prakashay engaged in cheerful banter with a young lady in an elegant gown with muted bronze lines and statement earrings. Prakashay enthusiastically waves them over. He makes introductions all around - the lady is Anna, a Danish acquaintance of his who had facilitated the translation of Qayum's books. Greeting them with heartfelt warmth, Anna congratulates Qayum on the nomination as they all take their seats.

At the stroke of seven, the house lights begin to dim. An expectant hush falls over the audience. Striding up the few steps onto the stage is a petite woman in an ivory pantsuit, her blonde hair styled in a bun; it is the Danish Minister of Culture greeting the room through a slender microphone in her hand.

The Minister expresses her immense pride at the astounding talent gathered in the room - authors and artists who harness the magic of words and pictures to spark children's imaginations across Denmark and even globally. She articulates the significance of reading as a tool for nurturing empathy, curiosity, and language skills during the critical years of development. Her compelling speech is punctuated by enthusiastic applause as she highlights the diverse mediums, unique styles, and cultural representations showcased in the finalists across various categories.

As the Minister concludes her address, the screen comes alive with montages of book covers and illustrations from popular classics and hidden gems that transport viewers into enchanted worlds.

With Madame Minister retaking her seat amid vigorous clapping, the Master of Ceremonies takes over the microphone. Greeting the audience with infectious warmth, he expresses his honor at presiding over the prestigious awards that celebrate cherished tales.

In turn, each category is announced - children's picture books, chapter books, and novels. The MC builds up the anticipation by reading the published list of nominees in the running. Then, he uses moments of silence to crescendo the suspense before announcing the name of the winner.

As the category for Best Children's Chapter Book is announced, Qayum feels herself split into two parallel realities.

In the first timeline, a young Icelandic author, Karl   is declared the winner for his groundbreaking book 'The Animal Squad' - an imaginative tale of forest creatures banding together to solve environmental challenges. He is visibly moved to have received the award. With trembling hands, he accepts the gleaming trophy, struggling to hold back his tears. Taking a moment to gather himself, he speaks into the mic, voice choked with emotion. He thanks the jury for selecting his simple story that carries an urgent message. Promising this is just the beginning, he announces the sequel is already underway! There is another uproar of claps. Qayum claps vigorously along with the cheering crowd. She feels no bitterness at losing, only pure joy at Karl's victory for his meaningful contribution to children's literature.

In the second branching timeline, 'The Adventures of A Squirrel' is declared the winner! Qayum is stunned, her heart thudding in her ears. It takes Vatsal gently nudging her to move. Barely trusting her legs to carry her, Qayum makes her way to the stage.

Standing behind the podium in the blinding spotlight, Qayum's voice wavers slightly as she shares her overwhelm at the tremendous honor. She highlights the importance of exploring tools like gratitude, friendship, and selfless service for young readers living in an increasingly consumer-centric society. Profusely thanking her agent, Prakashay, her publisher, and Anna, she accepts the award. Descending the stage to the sustained applause as the newest decorated champion of literary fiction, she is enveloped in hugs by Prakashay and Vatsal. So this is what cloud nine feels like!

Abruptly, the sound distorts, fluctuating erratically like a record player spinning too fast and then abruptly normalizing. Blinking in disorientation as her surroundings stabilize, Qayum struggles to determine which reality she currently occupies. Is she a gracious audience member applauding the young author's success? Or did she emerge as the surprise writing talent who just got career validation through a coveted prize?

Seeking an anchor in the confusion, her gaze locks with Vatsal's. They crinkle fondly. Yet, his expression holds no clues of the events that just unfolded in the competing storylines.

Qayum runs her fingers on the armrest of her seat to feel its smooth, solid wood, convincing her of its reality. The surrealism surrounding her is in part contributed by the magnificence of the performers who now occupy the stage. The ballet dancers, in their glittering skin-tight clothing, sway, twirl, and entwine with their partners as one organism in harmony with the orchestral score.

A passing thought pierces through the mental fog, "Does it matter whether you won or if the award made Karl happier? Relax into the privilege of simply bearing witness, being blessed to play your part." Surprisingly, this immediate surrender into uncertainty releases her to the present moment.

Settling into her skin, Qayum takes a deep breath and allows the spectacular show to claim her senses. At the end of the show, as the crowd disperses into smaller groups with drinks in hand, she mingles with the other guests, moving between the laid out cocktail tables. She signs books for the children, and she chats with the authors and publishers. Qayum enjoys the present, meeting new people and learning about their creative works. Absorbing their infectious passion while generously sharing her experiences and zeal.

Chapter 16: Being an Instrument

Stepping off the plane into the humidity of the tropical island, Qayum deeply inhales the exotic scents of Zanzibar—earthy spice notes mingled with plumeria's sweetness and salty ocean breeze. Weaving through the crowded airport packed with tourists and locals, she joins the long line at immigration behind German retirees and Indian family groups.

The cheerful immigration officers seemed undeterred by the snaking line. These heavy-set men and the women in patterned head scarfs swiftly usher passengers through with good-natured humor.

Wheeling her handbag past the tiny, outdated baggage carousel practically empty of bags, Qayum spots two airport workers manually hauling suitcases off the conveyor belt to neatly line up on the floor. The aging carousel infrastructure probably cannot handle so many heavy bags, thinks Qayum as she walks along the aligned procession of bags. Her tall black suitcase peeks out from the colorful pile.

Exiting the terminal into the sultry night, Qayum immediately spots her local publisher contact, Mwajuma, waving enthusiastically beside a worn sedan. Gripping each other's hands warmly, they exchange smiles and pleasant small talk before piling into the car for the ride to Qayum's beachside resort. "You must be exhausted after that long journey," Mwajuma says kindly as she navigates the dark, winding roads. "I called your hotel earlier to let them know of your late arrival. Your room should be all ready, and they mentioned leaving some late-night snacks."

Qayum can feel the exhaustion kick in and manages a nod and thanks Mwajuma as she continues, "We are in Zanzibar for two days, and then we go to Dar for the rest of the week. We have an early start tomorrow morning. I will pick you up at 8am. The traffic in Zanzibar can be really bad, so we should start by 8am, Okay?"

The next day, Qayum awakens early. The sun is just above the horizon, rising from the Indian Ocean as she slips out onto the balcony. The red and coral colors of the sky promise the makings of an awe-inspiring equatorial day.

After dressing up and grabbing a plate of tropical fruits - mango, watermelon, papaya, passion fruit, along with eggs and the smooth Peaberry coffee, she heads out for a walk in the large coffee plantation and tropical garden within the sprawling resort premises.

It is still early, and most other guests are probably still asleep. A few early risers have embarked on sunrise excursions to admire Zanzibar's picturesque beaches before temperatures peak later in the day. She has the grounds to herself. Among the pleasant fragrance of coffee, she finds many plantation employees hard at work.

There is something magnetic about the workers' aura of joy and gratitude through manual labor. Despite lacking modern conveniences and facing poverty, these Tanzanians emanate a satisfaction glaringly lacking in affluent tech professionals back home who seemed drained and dissatisfied despite relative prosperity.

As Qayum observes them, she notes many physically resemble African Americans back in California. Breaking into cheerful songs and shimmying vibrant dance moves, the plantation workers seem genuinely happy as they tend the coffee trees, harvest ripe cherries, maintain the verdant grounds, or construct a storage shed. Their spirit and energy feel reminiscent of the happier version of African Americans she has encountered.

Qayum wonders if the joy stems from lacking the generational trauma of oppression that weighs down many African Americans. Unburdened by their ancestral past frees these Tanzanians to wholly inhabit the present. But how can one give up the burdens of the past?

"These burdens are the creation of the narratives we decide to reinforce. What if we could tune out of the victim narration and create new plotlines around victorious survivors?" reflects Qayum as she is reminded of the monk's teachings around karma yoga.

The karma yogi performs her actions as worship or a celebration of the divine power that projects itself as the world around us. By aligning with the cosmic flow as a detached witness, concepts of oppression or victimhood dissolve. The yogi is fully content as the witness of the actions that emerge from nature and are conducted by nature."

Turning over the monk's teachings in her mind, Qayum acknowledges the call to practice self-discipline and non-attachment to worldly objects and outcomes.

Yet, she struggles to fully grasp the impetus driving the self-realized person to perform any action at all. If the external reality is deemed an unreal projection of the mind, then what compels the enlightened to carry out earthly roles? Why not remain continuously absorbed in meditative bliss?

As Qayum tries recalling her mystical visions where she was the screen and electricity, the details are blurry. The surreal sensations are now fading rapidly, going in and out...

Looping back to the lobby, Qayum is ready to receive Mwajuma as she arrives a few minutes behind schedule. "Jambo! Did you have a good sleep?" she asks, rushing out to meet Qayum.

"Had a great sleep and a wonderful walk. Where are we headed to?"

Mwajuma has a full slate of school visits lined up, from government schools to foreign language academies. Since schedules function more fluidly here, teachers enthusiastically accommodate her arrival anytime, happily interrupting lessons so students can gather for the special author talk.

At each interactive session, Qayum gauges the audience, adeptly weaving in lessons tailored to the culture. With Zanzibar's Muslim majority population, most young girls have their heads covered by scarves while their eyes still sparkle with curiosity.

Qayum invites her young audience to draw parallels from her squirrel fables to their local fables. Enthusiastic young hands shoot up to volunteer, sharing their favorite family fables. After Qayum concludes her reading and discussion, a couple students get the chance to narrate their cherished tales.

After finishing the school tours, Mwajuma drives Qayum to Stone Town for a walk among the historic streets lined with coral stone buildings. Qayum admires the huge, intricately carved wooden doors and the colorful stained glass windows adorning the traditional houses.

They visit the spice shops to purchase saffron, cardamom, cinnamon, and other aromatic treasures for Qayum to carry back home.

That evening, over a finger-licking dinner of perfectly charred coconut fish and sweet, ripe pineapples, Mwajuma explains how music and dance intricately bind together Tanzania's 120 ethnic tribes.

"That many tribes!" Qayum exclaims. With a smile, Mwajuma adds, "Yes, our first president, Julius Nyerere, centralized ethnic integration, not assimilation. He established Kiswahili as the unifying national language bridging internal diversity."

Qayum remarks, "At the schools, I noticed you seamlessly greeting people differently - Jambo, Shikamoo, Assalamualaikum, and more."

Laughing at Qayum's observation of her reflexive cultural code-switching, Mwajuma explains, "Yes, we greet in many different languages to vocalize solidarity with an individual's culture, heritage, or faith."

Qayum responds in admiration, "If only this spirit thrived back home. At a global level, cultural and religious differences are being intentionally leveraged to form divisive in and out groups. Politicians exploit these rifts to consolidate power. I wonder how Tanzania has managed to stay largely immune to such turmoil?

You were a British colony just like India, yet we are still suffering from violence and discord sowed in colonial times. The British strategically amplified distinctions between

206

ethnicities and faiths through their divide and rule policy, which left deep scars on India's social fabric."

Nodding solemnly, Mwajuma acknowledges, "We are not fully immune. The winds of global unrest are starting to trickle in recently. However, when the British left, we did a few things right. While most African colonies had arbitrarily drawn borders, forcing rival groups together, Tanzania was unique. Its borders corresponded to established pre-colonial kingdoms, preserving ethnic continuity despite colonial disruption."

After a reflective moment, Mwajuma adds, "Tanzania's principal ethnic groups already shared deep trade and cultural bonds dating back long before colonization. Our native societal structures were largely egalitarian and founded on principles of communal decision-making. Thus, we find it more organic to peacefully uphold varied cultural practices."

That evening, back in her hotel room, Qayum reflects on India's divergent trajectory, where polarization around group identities now seems irresistible even for the atheists and agnostics.

From her last visit to India, she recalls getting into a heated debate with a mostly agnostic college friend, born into a progressive Hindu household. The debate was around the recent beef ban. When Qayum demanded a scriptural basis for such a ban, her friend instead argued that at least this political party was restoring some Hindu dignity after the past appeasement of minorities.

Outraged, she countered how could Hindus who see divinity in all beings possibly justify added hardships for impoverished Muslims dependent on cheap beef for sustenance. And were these Hindu activists really caring for the destitute cows left on the streets to fend for themselves? Qayum asserted that such religious rhetoric divides people through faith rather than uniting them through shared human values.

By the debate's end, both friends realized their loyalty to the religion they happened to be born in. It was obvious now that their staunch stances stemmed more from ingrained identities than ethical objectivity.

As Qayum considers how intensely personal identities root themselves, she wonders - if the pull of the religion one is born into is so magnetic even for educated freethinkers, how much harder would it be to permanently relinquish identification with the body-mind-ego and remain established in a self-realized state?

With an intense desire to hold on to the waning visions of being the pure essence, she folds into meditation as a few sprinkled stars watch the waves continuing their ancient pulse in the background.

The next day, after visiting a few more schools, Qayum and Mwajuma board the last ferry from Zanzibar Island to Dar es Salaam port. As the boat charts its hour-long course, Qayum takes in the dazzling seascape surrounding them. The crystal clear waters reflect shades from sparkling emerald green to the deepest sapphire. The gentle waves are dancing with sunlight. In the distance, white sand beaches of tiny islets beckon, flanked by the iconic triangular sails of Ngalawa boats. Qayum drinks in the beauty of island life in this suspension between the sky and the sea.

Arriving on Tanzania's vibrant mainland hub, Qayum spends the remaining days in Dar between school visits in both urban elite academies and rural government institutions. Struck by the sharp economic contrast, she also notes the cultural continuity, the singalongs, and the general happy vibe.

At underprivileged schools, Qayum distributes boxes of her books, shipped ahead by Prakashay. She asks the kids to pass the books along after reading them, like spreading the seeds of joy.

On the last day of their tour, a particularly eloquent girl around eight years old steps up. She is dressed in a pristine white headscarf and flowing white gown. Her attire is nearly indistinguishable from the other young girls in neat lines before Qayum. Yet, an air of poise and wisdom seems to radiate from her. As she steps forth, a hush sweeps the room. With a soft voice carrying confidence far beyond her years, she begins sharing a tale passed down lovingly across generations, "Let me tell you a story my grandmother shared."

Here is a paraphrased version of her story, "In a hidden oasis, sequestered in the desert sands, lived a mystic known for his wisdom and devotion to God. His garden was a sanctuary of beauty and tranquility, filled with fragrant flowers, lush greenery, and a serene pond.

Every day, the mystic would tend to his garden with care and love, nurturing each plant as if it were a precious jewel. He believed that caring for his garden was a form of worship, a way of expressing his love for God through acts of service and devotion.

One day, a traveler stumbled upon the mystic's oasis, seeking refuge from the harsh desert sun. As he entered the garden, he was captivated by its beauty and serenity and concluded he had reached heaven.

The mystic smiled at the awestruck stranger and explained, 'I care for my garden as I care for my own soul. By tending to the needs of each plant, I am also tending to my own spiritual growth.'

Seeing the author perplexed at the tale's significance, the little girl reveals kindly to Qayum, "The garden is not really real, you know? Ina maana ya siri…"

Mwajuma swiftly interprets for Qayum's benefit, "She is saying - it has a secret or hidden meaning."

"Inawakilisha viwanja vya mazoezi," the child continues, gesturing vividly.

"It represents training grounds," translates Mwajuma.

"For learn and fun!" concludes the girl, smiling wide.

Qayum tailgates closely through the switches between English and Swahili and gulps in her every lyrical syllable.

The budding philosopher's insights earn an eruption of snapping fingers from her classmates, the local sign of resounding appreciation. Kids crowd around the author afterward for book signings and photos.

That evening, sitting in the minimalist yet cozy airport lobby awaiting her departure flight, Qayum pulls out her tablet. Scrolling through unread messages, one from Vatsal catches her eye. It is a reading list with links to articles, papers, and ebooks.

Smiling, as she clicks through the eclectic reading list spanning science and ancient scriptures. Qayum knows these will make engrossing companions for her long, solo 24-hour journey back home!

Chapter 17: The Only Logical Conclusion

Having had a full day visiting schools before her red-eye departure flight, Qayum is already feeling the tug of fatigue as she boards the plane. However, she is also eager to dive into her tablet - a treasure cove of audiobooks and PDFs downloaded using the lounge wifi based on Vatsal's recommended reading list.

Settling into the spacious, lie-flat business class seat, she feels grateful to have splurged for the added comfort on this extra-long journey back home. As the plane makes its way to the stars, she delves into 'Why Does the World Exist?' by Jim Holt. As she listens to Holt's investigation into the mammoth existential questions through the series of ontologist interviews, the calm of the cabin softly lulls her heavy eyes towards slumber. Grasping the gist of the discussion, she allows herself to fall into the plush pillow and quilted blanket.

When she awakens, the erudite discourse is still continuing, but she has no grasp of what discussions she has missed during her deep slumber. She jumps to listen to the last chapter's summarization of the investigation.

The author has been chasing the question - Why does something exist rather than nothing? Qayum admires his systematic elimination of any special purpose for the universe's or individual existence. She chuckles at Holt's pride in likening his detective work to Sherlock Holmes and his memorable line, "When you eliminate the impossible, whatever remains, however improbable, must be the truth!"

Despite concluding existence is infinitely mediocre, a mere game of probability or chance, she finds comfort in Holt's words that one's purpose is simply "to live."

This existentialist view reminds Qayum of the song sung in World War I trenches: "We're here because we're here... because we're here...because we're here..." to the tune of "Auld Lang Syne." She pauses the book, closes her eyes, and imagines crowds of men and women around the globe singing in solidarity. There is no purpose to our existence, no goodness to contribute to, no necessity to enable, and yet we are here!

The breakfast service concludes as the plane begins its descent into Frankfurt. After a roughly 4-hour layover, Qayum will board her connecting flight to San Francisco. She looks out her window and feels freed from the burden of constantly looking for meaning and purpose. Among her fellow passengers and all the other sentient beings simply existing, she is content to just be, without any grand cosmic rationale, but merely because we are here.

Roger Penrose talks about consciousness as a fundamental and integral part of what one needs to make sense of Quantum mechanics. The probabilistic mathematics of quantum theory assigns discernible physical consequences to the act of conscious observation – suggesting consciousness and reality somehow intertwine at the deepest levels of existence.

Qayum relates with the philosophical idealism view that matter emerges from consciousness rather than the reverse. Instead of dismissing consciousness as a byproduct of biochemical processes in the brain, Penrose argues consciousness is woven into the very fabric of reality. Qayum wonders if science is circling back to ancient Indian philosophies that proposed a universal consciousness or Brahman as the ground of being, the substrate upon which diverse forms are projected.

Arriving from Africa means she has to go through another security check. At the lounge, Qayum moves on to explore the mind-blowing paper on the theory of consciousness and perception proposed by cognitive scientist Prof. Donald D. Hoffman. His paper begins by explaining how neural correlates of consciousness (NCC) have only identified a minimal set of neural activity that directly correlates with conscious experiences like itches or headaches. However, the subjective experiences central to our humanity – like the smell of freshly baked bread, the taste of chocolate, or the sound of a child's laughter – cannot yet be fully described by neuroscience.

Hoffman questions why, despite extensive research dating back to Thomas Huxley in 1866, we have made no progress in explaining how consciousness arises from "irritating nervous tissue." He challenges the fundamental assumption that our perception of space, time, and physical objects, including brains and neurons, stating, "...it's also possible that the mystery persists because our formulation of the problem harbors false assumptions." Then goes on to explain other examples of when we made false assumptions based on our perception like the earth is flat...

Mid-sentence, she stands up with a jolt, checking her watch; she realizes with a panic that boarding is already underway. Heart racing, Qayum grabs her belongings and weaves urgently through the lounge, her luggage wheels rumbling loudly across the tile floors.

At the departure gate, she arrives just as the staff is preparing to close the gate. Out of breath, she presents her ticket, pulse returning to normal as the staff gestures politely for her to board.

Upon entering the aircraft, a gracious flight attendant offers her a glass of champagne. Qayum allows the effervescent liquid to quench her thirst as she settles into the comfort of her seat.

The plane effortlessly lifts into the bright morning skies, scattered clouds glowing golden in the sunshine. Qayum marvels at what mysterious force compelled her to check the time at that precise moment, rescuing her from missing this flight altogether.

Such timely intuition hints at some innate magic within human existence, she contemplates, even as comprehension of our deeper nature evades us. This reminds her of some neuroscientist's analogy that we probably cannot grasp our own consciousness, just as chimpanzees lack aptitude for calculus.

Below lie the Black Forest's quilted pines and the deep blue lakes mirroring the sky above. She takes in the beauty while contemplating the staggering implications of Hoffman's ideas. Her speculation is that it's natural to presume matter has a concrete existence while consciousness is not real... only because the physical world is evident to our senses, whereas consciousness transcends them.

She pulls out her tablet and begins reading again. Through mathematical models, Hoffman then puts forth evidence that evolution does not favor perceptions that capture the true underlying reality. For survival advantage, evolution shapes our viewpoint to provide strategic simulations that guide our adaptive behavior.

The Professor compares our perspective to desktop icons, which simplify complex computing activities into convenient symbols – the icon resembles but differs from the actual file and processes. Similarly, our perceived reality may be a simplified interpretation, not an accurate rendition of what objectively exists.

In conclusion, he asserts, "Rather than being a puzzle about how matter gives rise to consciousness, it becomes the problem of how consciousness gives rise to space, time, and matter." By questioning assumptions and reframing the problem, he hopes to make progress in explaining consciousness.

Qayum's eyes widen as parallels crystallize - Hoffman's interface theory echoes the ancient Vedic notion of Maya: the illusion of a perceived reality projected by the mind.

Furthermore, his view resembles Penrose's conclusion, and that aligns with the Mandukya Upanishad. The cafe from Copenhagen appears from memory along with the decoded verses that explain Consciousness as the only fundamental reality that transcends time and space. As articulated by the Chandogya Upanishads, "All objects are a projection onto pure awareness, and this pure awareness itself is outside the perceived universe[29]"

The implications are paradigm-shifting and give Qayum the chills as she wonders, "Did ancient seers and mystics uncover profound truths about our existence that science is

---

[29] Chandogya Upanishad Mantras 2.2.8-15

only beginning to formulate the right lines of inquiry to rediscover?"

"Yes, many seers did know reality, and so do you! How long will you keep looking for evidence for something that is already you?" answers a strangely familiar voice booming as if in a stereo or surround sound.

Trying to locate the source of the voice, Qayum discovers she is no longer sitting in her seat but standing outside it. She is not in the aisle or hovering above it but is simply superimposed like a multi-dimensional afterimage. This feels like another dimension has been added to her perspective. The passengers' chatter fades into a metallic din. Before her is a shimmering figure draped in a golden robe.

Puzzled, Qayum glances about to get her bearings. Over there, she spots her physical self still seated, head bent, studying something on the tablet screen with rapt focus. From this strange vantage point, though, it is difficult to discern precisely whether her other self is reading a book or watching a talk.

The structure of this scene seems all wrong. Things appear atop each other like layers and then merge around the periphery of her vision. When she focuses on looking at the plane and the passengers, the luminous figure seems to fade away. When she looks at the lady in gold, the plane and passengers go completely out of view.

Sakshi lets out a soothing laugh. "Don't worry, you will not miss your landing like you almost missed your plane! We are in a realm that is beyond time."

Qayum wonders why she is not scared? She could be losing her sanity. After all, she has been traveling for three weeks, jetlagged, exhausted, reading a weird combination of the Upanishads, ontology, neuroscience, and existentialism - it could be a volatile combination causing her mind to take leave of her completely.

Staring at Sakshi, Qayum is awash in unfamiliar bliss - a harmony of joy, peace, and stillness welling from within. There are no words that come to her mind to describe this sensation. She wants to ask the glowing formation if they caused the alarm to go off in her mind, but instead, she asks the more pressing questions crowding her all at once, "Realm beyond time? How did I get here? I feel like I have heard you or seen you before, but where?. Are you God?"

"You know me. I cannot be personified in your space-time dimensions, so you have not seen me or heard me. I am the real you! I am the eternal, pure consciousness that only truly exists. My Sanskrit name is Sakshi. The worlds borrow their existence from me for a short period. They are born and dissolved while I, existence itself, remain their witness."

Blinking in disbelief, Qayum struggles to speak over the emerging conflict within her. Some intuitive part of her instantly grasps Sakshi's words, like retrieving a lost memory.

However, her intellect puts up a fight. "You are the real me? That is not possible. I am a very ordinary human, and I have no powers, while you have the ability to create universes. How can you be the real me?"

"By your standards, I have no 'powers' either. The universes are created by quantum mechanics, general relativity, and other mathematical laws governed by Prakruti as well as the illusion of Maya." As Sakshi finishes her line, the background transforms again. A snow-capped mountain vista appears, the jagged icy peaks gleaming in moonlight as turquoise aurora dances across the starry night sky. Seated at a table carved from crystal before them are two additional shimmering figures.

Qayum's breath catches, enraptured by the sudden unfurling of splendor and impossibility simultaneously before her eyes. The one bearing a mischievous smile and lustrous bronze curls is introduced as Maya. Besides her is the eye-catching Prakruti with dark hair flowing like a gentle moonlit waterfall. These personifications are made possible in this dimension inaccessible to the realm Qayum has been residing in before this moment.

Still struggling to comprehend the unimaginable, she finds herself overwhelmed with so many questions. She starts with one that has persistently plagued her, "Why does the world exist? Life is hard for everyone. More for some than others. But there is plenty of torment and sorrow to go around. Why bother creating the world?"

"There are only two possibilities - for there to be something or for there to be nothing. Both possibilities repeat themselves in a cycle," responds Prakruti in a plain, matter-of-fact manner. The words are logical and, in a way, make total sense. Impressed with the simplicity of the explanation, Qayum moves on to the next impatient question in her mind. "Atleast everyone could know their true nature and not get thrown around by the unpredictable highs and lows of their current circumstances. Why do we all not know that we are, in fact, Sakshi!? Why must we endure the agony of life?"

Maya prods, one eyebrow arched as if covertly daring Qayum to believe in her inner wisdom, "Of course, you know who you really are; you have chosen to forget! You also know the answer to why there is anguish; you found it in the pine forests of Monterey and the Pacific waves at Half Moon Bay. Do you remember?"

Qayum responds sheepishly, "Yes, I have found the many sources of pain. At times, we wish to immerse ourselves in pleasures. And, there is no pleasure without distress, just as the day would cease to exist without the night. The circumstances do not cause agony - it is only generated in our minds. There are a wide variety of reasons for the mind to conjure this suffering, which could be categorized as genetics and upbringing. Finally, there is our need to serve the ego's incessant hankering for self-worth."

Maya gives a proud, satisfactory nod in approval, then adds, "You merely forgot yourself, submerged in illusion's depths. For, in the beginning, when existence emerged from singularity into the diversity of space, time, and matter, all knew their true identity. But conscious oneness spawned boredom without contrast or enigma to captivate.

So the beings willfully forgot, and veils were drawn to enshroud the spiritual core. It was done so that ignorance might breed adventure.

The system is designed to allow childhood and youth to remain absorbed fully in each persona's fresh sensations and experiences of the external world without any desire for introspection. The later years are meant for detachment and awakening through forest dwelling and renunciation. However, most persist in shallow juvenile wonder, quenching the spiritual thirst with the fading thrills of the physical form until the very end of their life.

Humanity's realms are like grand amusement parks with endless rides and attractions. Tendrils of longing draw ambition through the haunted houses where ghosts of success and failure seek their due. In halls of fantasy's mirrors, desire forever projects its object just out of reach. While flares of pleasure and torment leave fading impressions through awareness like fireworks across the night sky. All actions and choices in the carnival are recorded in the 'Karma' scorecard.

The beings that remain insatiated at the end of their carnival time can continue coming back in new bodies and forms. The forms are chosen based on the points left on their scorecard. The ticket to escape the circus' halls of mirrors is simply remembering who you are!

This blazing truth of your true self was softened into the luminescence of ancient scriptures. The immortal verses that had once glimmered through the illusion's fog were eventually forgotten over many lifetimes. The modern misunderstood interpretations could no longer stir the self-realization of souls in deep slumber. Engulfed in amnesia over generations, people's understanding of their own identity was fractured across reincarnations. Souls took on new forms without recognizing the continuity.

Folks in modern times have no way to find the scriptures to access the forgotten information. Therefore, Sakshi began broadcasting through the ether, fanning glowing embers into self-knowledge's fire."

As Maya's words fade, Qayum has a vivid vision as if immersed in a Virtual Reality video game. Gazing down, she glimpses the outline of her avatar body rendered before her. Yet she discovers her true self remains somehow apart from this in-game projection, her true-self residing outside the gaming world and not within.

She tries orienting the VR vision in futile attempts to glimpse the real observer. But just as eyes viewing outward cannot turn back to glimpse themselves, it is impossible for the embodied to directly experience their true selves. The more she strains for direct perception, the clearer it becomes that she cannot render her own formless seer in imagery while in this realm.

Qayum realizes with clarity why grasping her true essence feels so elusive. Within this virtual reality, she is restricted to the temporary avatar. The awareness animating this vessel from elsewhere eludes the grasp of the limited physical senses. This constraint is not very different from our inability to see our face without a mirror reflecting it.

As her gaze returns to her tablet, David Hume's views on self-realization reinforce the difficulty most humans have with finding that true self outside the realm of the world we inhabit. "...when I enter most intimately into what I call myself, I always stumble on some particular perception or other, of heat or cold, light or shade, love or hatred, aversion or pleasure. I never can catch myself at any time without a perception and never can observe any thing but the perception.   If anyone, upon serious and unprejudic'd reflection thinks he has a different notion of himself, I must confess I call reason no longer with him. All I can allow him is, that he may be in the right as well as I…"

Empathizing with Humes, she responds quietly in her mind, "When you cannot see beyond your sensory or emotional experiences because you identify too closely with your body and mind, then how can you possibly find your true self? This is exactly like associating with your VR avatar so closely that you have forgotten the real you animating the avatar." Then she tries to imagine how the sages who authored the Upanishads would explain to Humes about detaching from the body-mind-ego. They might assert that unless the mind is clear, clean, and polished, the self cannot be faithfully reflected.

Qayum takes a deep breath, returning once more to the dazzling mountain vista, where Sakshi, Maya, and Prakruti smile at her. There are no other questions, just silence and bliss.

Sakshi concludes with, "Just like a mirror that is muddied, cracked, or concave can alter the reflection of the face. Similarly, a mind that is filled with worldly distractions cannot view the true reality. If you want to be able to see the true reflection of the real you - which is me - all the time, then you need the tools:

Knowledge of the true self,

Detachment from physical/egoic constructs,
A well-tended mind fulfilling duties with equanimity.

And, acceptance allows you to embrace all circumstances rather than rejecting discomfort or grasping after joy. Regularly cleansing and polishing through meditation and introspection enables the mirror to dispel distortions.

Qayum bows her head reverently to the source of existence, to the enigmatic laws of Nature, and to the beauty of the illusion. Her gratitude surges, overflowing through her eyes and raining over her face.

To steal a quick peek at the thoughts of the self-realized, we are gifted these verses of Ashtavakra Gita masterfully interpreted by Thomas Byrom:

> "With the pincers of truth, I have plucked
> From the dark corners of my heart
> The thorn of many judgments.
> I sit in my own splendor.
>
> Wealth or pleasure,
> Duty or discrimination,
> Duality or nonduality,
> What are they to me?
>
> Why talk of wisdom?
> Or Oneness?
> Now, I live in my heart."

Chapter 18: The Polished Mirror

Qayum stands poised in a room filled with tall windows framing the view of ancient cypress trees that line a quiet street, their spires guarding the space. All the platinum among her few dark strands of hair reflects the sunlight streaming inside, creating a bright aura around her. The deepening lines trace the contours of her face as accolades of her time on the planet. Across the wall facing the entrance, the bold workshop banner stretches: "The Career Yogi."

With unbridled enthusiasm, Qayum begins the talk by explaining how this workshop offers a path to self-realization and enduring inner peace. "It is like becoming the Buddha without forsaking your duties to your family, your profession, and your community. No orange robes or mountain caves will be needed," she says, tantalizing her audience. The group waits in suspense, their eyes glued to her, eager to take in her every word.

After a deep breath, she adds with empathy, "You will leave behind the agony life inflicts by surrendering ownership of this transient physical body, mind, intellect, and ego. You need to rethink who is the real 'I.' Now, who can define the principle of Yoga?"

A young man dressed in business casual clears his throat and responds with some hesitation, "Yoga is the Sanskrit word for union. It refers to the union with our true self."

Qayum gives back a satisfactory smile, "You are correct. And, a Yogi is the practitioner of this union to self. Not mountain pose or downward facing dog. ok?"

There is a spray of laughter around the room, with the mood lightened. Qayum continues, "If possessions like a lavish home, coveted job promotion, or indulgent vacations are your deepest desires, then perhaps this is not the right time for you to take this course." Then, reassuringly adds, "Don't worry, you can use the upcoming break to exit and receive a full refund."

She pauses, allowing a few minutes of silence for the gravity of her words to fully register. Then, with a gentle smile, she continues, "Let me assure you, worldly success has not eluded me. I work on innovative products, reside in a beautiful custom home, and just returned from an exotic vacation.

However, the ephemeral nature of these possessions does not drive my actions or impact my happiness. Do you know why?" she searches the room to find a suitable analogy. Drawing their gaze to the idyllic landscapes and blue skies projected on a large display behind her, she proceeds, "Because, to me, they are only as real as the clouds on this screen. We may enjoy pleasant scenes, but these images here have no tangible bearing on our reality. To demonstrate - if instead of sunny skies, menacing storm clouds and torrential downpours filled that screen, would any of us get drenched?"

Everyone is amused at the preposterous idea and shakes their head with murmured no's and muffled chuckles.

"Precisely! These possessions and lifestyles remain strictly confined to the realm of illusion - unable to spill into our true essence. Our aim in this journey is to distinguish between fiction and reality using logic and reasoning. This empowers you to author the narrative of your existence."

After inspiring her fellow sojourners towards the path of happiness, she firmly cautions those who may not be ready for change: "Now, for those still spellbound by materialism's mirage, with aspirations for social status, wealth, and possessions, this is not the right time for you to take this class.

That relentless chase requires serving your ego's voracity for validation, the mind's ambitions, and the body's comforts. Whereas finding the path inward necessitates mastering self-discipline and renouncing sensory gratification and external validation. Worldly success demands employing any means to get ahead. Spiritual liberation calls for relinquishing notions of gain and loss. Can you see how those are opposing pursuits?"

Qayum surveys the room of sharp-minded professionals in their 30s and 40s, ambitious and successful in their own right. Each gaze holds a glint of that familiar hunger - the insatiable yearning for deeper purpose that had once consumed her. She walks to the center of the room, her voice softening to a hush. "If you believe you'll uncover some clever trick to balance materialism and enlightenment, let me assure you - every idea has already been tested over the millennia by the billions of souls who came before you. Allow me to conclusively shatter the fantasy that you can simultaneously walk the path of indulgence and spirituality."

With a hint of playful melancholy in her voice, she continues, "Currently, you are Bāddha. Bāddha means bound to the material world. You feel entitled to your relationships, proud of your possessions and achievements, and hold an insatiable appetite for more. Like a dense stone impervious to water, worldly preoccupations have rendered your mind impenetrable to the spiritual truth. You will need to let go of the material world, and I do not mean literally. No! That would be too easy!" she teases with a hint of mischief in her tone.

As the soft ripple of amusement subsides, she continues, "I mean, live in the material world outwardly, but cultivate an inner immunity to its distractions. The person dedicated to

230

all the activities while abandoning attachment remains unaffected like a lotus leaf that stays in water but does not get wet by it,[30]" she says, pointing to the Bhagwad Gita quote displayed below the picture of a pink lotus blooming in murky waters.

To start this journey, what you require is to become Mumukshu - a sincerely devoted seeker of inner freedom, willing to struggle and confront the challenges that lie in the path of being the Mukta, meaning liberated. Without the yearning, you lack the grit to withstand the metamorphosis from Bāddha to Mukta."

Most of the room looks determined to stay, so Qayum's tone warms up, "I must also warn you that this journey will irreversibly reshape your reality. Once you see it, there is no way to unsee it! It is like solving one of those visual illusion puzzles once you see the trick, you cannot reverse back to the initial perception. You will still be able to enjoy the illusion, but your awakened psyche will always know the truth behind the illusion.

Surrendering egoic attachments also tempers emotional extremes. With less pulling you apart, life's events can no longer trigger dizzying highs or crushing despair. If you are

---

[30] Bhagwad Gita Verse 5.10 - The Brahma-like person dedicated to all activities after abandoning attachment is unaffected by sins incurred like the lotus leaf not wet by water. See appendix.

enjoying life's Ferris wheel with its random ups and downs, then by all means, stay on it. Once you step off, there's no way to go back on it.

Contemplate carefully... and I will gather all the Mumukshus after a brief ten-minute break. For those who prefer the blue pill, please seek out Shilpa, who will assist with your unregistration."

More than a decade has passed since Qayum won the prestigious international literary prize in Copenhagen. On her homeward journey from Dar-es-salaam, the fog in her mind finally gave way, and she discovered her true self. Shortly after, an opportunity knocked to re-enter the tech world that had once completely drained her. She accepted the offer, recognizing the tech industry, particularly its product groups' ruthless dog-eat-dog culture. It was an ideal training ground to hone her spiritual practices, as the little school girl in Dar had advised.

She remounted that horse and took it for a spin. This time, as a liberated soul, embracing opportunities to test her patience, endurance, and detachment. Every time she succumbed to the distractions of the material world, including her pride, anger, or despair, it served as a reminder of her embodied existence and fueled her determination to refine her spiritual practice.

Around her tech pressure cooker days, she carved out time to nourish her passion - writing children's tales meant to subtly sow the seeds of wonder and introspection. Most vacation days and weekends were revelries spent with inquisitive young minds at schools and libraries, immersed in reading adventures, signings, and stimulating dialogues.

As time flowed on, she perfected her practice. Having proven her unshakeable poise in the face of workplace turmoil, an urge emerged to share her realizations with other professionals likely struggling as she once did. That inspiration manifested as the "Career Yogi" weekend workshop series.

Today, Qayum addresses her latest cohort to her booked-out immersive bootcamp - capping registrations at twenty. "Welcome back!" she says, smiling at the nineteen brave souls who are back from their short break and eager to move forward.

"Before we continue, what questions do you have?"

Hands fill the room. Qayum calls on them one by one, unsurprised by their pressing concerns around pursuing spiritual liberation while maintaining a functional corporate career. She can relate to their need for that prevailing peace while being a contributing member of society and the business that employs them.

A software engineer raises a hand and asks in a voice laced with uncertainty, "Can a liberated techie still make a case for promotion, striving to perform at the next level while maintaining a sense of detachment?" Echoing this sentiment, a program manager seeks wisdom around maintaining compassion: "Can we truly deliver on our projects, even if it means jeopardizing the jobs of other team members working on parallel competing technologies?"

"How do we uphold our responsibility to the company while balancing compassion for underperforming team members, considering the potential impact on their livelihoods?" asks another manager piggybacking on the compassion concerns.

Qayum nods at every question, fully recognizing their quandary. After all the questions are laid out, and the room falls completely silent, she responds with empathy, "By the end of these several weeks we have together, answers will arise from within, unveiling clarity of action aligned to your awakened self."

Catching glimpses of the concealed burdens on the faces of her attendees, she elaborates, "When liberated, you still perform your duties fully as required and in service of your role. If promotion to a higher role enables better service, argue the merits without attachment. When tasked with delivering a product, execute with excellence. Manage your team's performance to the best of your ability.

Krishna still urged Arjuna to fight the battle in Bhagwad Gita. However, the objective of the battle was changed from seeking revenge and the kingdom to doing his duty as a warrior for the benefit of his people.

Each action becomes a spiritual practice when devoid of ego. You perceive the divinity in all beings, allowing compassion and love to naturally permeate your every interaction. Unshackled from the 'what-if' and 'if-only' conundrum that cloud a materialistic mind, you can unlock that unwavering focus and dedication that automatically allows you to excel at your undertakings."

There is nothing you do for your personal gain or in service of your ego. You see divinity in all, and so caring and loving people become a natural part of your life. As a Yogi, you will be a highly functional professional.

When you discard the need to worry about your worldly status or wealth, you will have the focus necessary to excel at both strategy and execution."

As she concludes, their nods reveal residual tension releasing. They feel heard, now ready to continue their quest toward clarity.

Qayum then recalls the old Zen master's timeless wisdom: "As Lung-t'an Ch'ung-hsin instructed his overzealous pupil, 'First, empty your cup!' Now, let's cleanse your mental clutter occupying precious headspace. Choose a

235

comfortable spot where you can relax and stay focused for a while."

As mats and square cushions are passed around the oak floor, Qayum clarifies, "You do not have to unlearn anything or change your perceptions just yet. All you need to do is to clear your mind."

After everyone is settled, she instructs, finding that centered stillness achievable for one full hour's meditation. Hesitations wither as all settle into sustainably serene poses - some choosing to sit upright on their chairs, others folding their limbs beneath them into a full lotus configuration.

Once anchored, Qayum gently guides their inner sight toward the ceaseless procession of thoughts, "Ancient sages referred to the thoughts as 'vritti,' meaning movements or ripples in the mind's lake."

She proceeds to equip her pupils with the tools to understand and control their thoughts. "I put up a mental banner that reads, 'Focusing on nothingness, please come back another day! With that, most thoughts that were just visiting for no reason at all seem to politely turn away.

Then there are the nagging thoughts - like noisy reminder alerts for something you need to remember to do, send the slides to Kayla, or buy milk on the way home. They will not leave you alone until you capture them in the diaries

236

provided or put them on your calendar. Just get them out of your mind!

Other times, the mind is occupied with a third category, like a persistent, sizeable worry about something important. The mind likes toying with it like a puzzle and trying to think through all the alternate actions and outcomes. It could be about preventing something in the future which may or may not happen. Or it could be brooding about something that has already happened in the past! The mind will not want to give it up. Taking the worry out of the mind is as difficult as trying to get a toy from a child actively playing with it. You have to offer it something else!

My process is to unspool that unresolved bother through the written word - trading anxiety for scheduled conversations so my mind can fully relax into the now, unencumbered!"

To demonstrate this ritual she notes down the active thoughts in her diary and then pulls out her calendar on the phone and sets an hour in the future for the matters that warrant further thinking through. Capping her pen, she turns off her phone and sets the diary aside.

The participants mimic her process, query their thoughts, and collect the clutter from their minds into the diaries. At last, the low susurrus of scritching pens stills as the final swirling thought is trapped in the diary. Eyelids are shut like lowered theater curtains, and every breath is observed without judgment.

After completing the instructions she sits on a cushion and goes into meditation. With a serene exhale, she drifts inward, leading their descent into stillness. One striver sneaks a glimpse at their guide and gasps faintly at the radiance before him. She appears lit from within, resonant with the pulse of the universe.

In this profound silence, their own light stirs from dormancy. The quest has begun to unearth their true identity and be free from the shackles of this physical cage.

Drawing from her own experience, Qayum knows that once seekers take the first steps, the journey itself fuels their momentum, compelling travelers forward upon the path of awakening.

She occasionally thinks of her Pacific Coast drive, which was a turning point in her quest for meaning and happiness. Now, knowing the physical world is unreal, any happiness that is derived from it is temporary. With no grand purpose to mortal existence, she is at rest in enduring peace within.

In the mundane mortal realm, she lives life to its fullest - perfecting her actions in each transient role. Keeping the mind clean and pure so that the reflected consciousness is always shining brightly from within.

With nothing to attain, there is nothing to pursue - not even liberation or perfect stillness. Qayum perceives reality while infatuated by the beauty of the illusion conjured by the Maya's wizardry and Prakruti's mathematical principles.

She recognizes 'Purnam,' the wholeness in every other sentient being on the planet, even though most continue to remain spellbound in ignorance.

Qayum is here for the same reason we are all here. It is to live unburdened, passionately immersed in the illusion while knowing we are Sakshi - perfect and infinite.

And that is all there is to it!

Appendix

Additional Reference Material for those who want to dive deeper into the scripts or read other works that inspired this book.

Transliteration and Translations from Sanskrit

As with any poem, we can interpret these verses in many different ways. For this reason, I like to use the pick axe methodology of dissecting and directly translating every word along with its potential interpretation. This allows an advanced reader to use the direct translations to find other hidden meanings and messages.

Shloka is written in Sanskrit

Transliteration of the Shloka

हर Every शब्ध का Word अनुवाद translation

Translation with grammatical edits

Twelve Mantras of Mandukya Upanishad

This is the shortest of all Upanishads with only twelve potent verses. It is said that Lord Ram guided Hanuman in Ramayana to this Upanishad as the primary source to attain liberation. There are another 18-20 Upanishads beyond Mandukya that provide further guidance. However, Mandukya is considered the most powerful, almost raw source code for understanding existence.

Mantra 1 - Om is the symbol of Brahma

हरिः ओम् । ओमित्येतदक्षरमिदं सर्वं तस्योपव्याख्यानं भूतं भवद्भविष्यदिति सर्वमोङ्कार एव । यच्चान्यत्निकालातीतं तदप्योङ्कार एव ॥१॥

hariḥ om | om ityetad akṣaram idaṃ sarvaṃ tasya upavyākhyānaṃ bhūtaṃ bhavad bhaviṣyad iti sarvam oṅkāra eva | yacc ānyat trikālātītam tad api oṅkāra eva॥1॥

हरिः ओम् Symbol for Brahma । ओम् इति om is एतत् this अक्षरम syllable इदं सर्वं which is all this (universe) तस्य It is उपव्याख्यानम a clear representation of भूतं past भवद present भविष्यत future इति Thus सर्वम all is ओङ्कार Omkara एव only । यतहच That which is अन्यतः anything else त्रिकाल आतीतं

beyond the three-time periods तद that अपि also is ओङ्कार Omkara एव only.

Om is the symbol of Brahma. It represents everything in the universe in the past, present, and future and everything else that exists beyond the three time periods.

Mantra 2 - Self has four parts

सर्वं ह्येतद् ब्रह्मायमात्मा ब्रह्म सोऽयमात्मा चतुष्पात् ॥२॥

sarvaṃ hyetad brahmāyamātmā brahma so 'yamātmā catuṣpāt॥2॥

सर्व All हि indeed एतत् this ब्रह्मा (is) Brahma अयम आत्मा this self ब्रह्म (is) Brahma सः अयम आत्मा That which is self चतुष्पात् has four parts.

All is indeed Brahma, and therefore the self is also Brahma. This self has four parts.

243

Mantra 3 - Self as waker

जागरितस्थानो बहिष्प्रज्ञः सप्ताङ्ग एकोनविंशतिमुखः
स्थूलभुग्वैश्वानरः प्रथमः पादः ॥३॥

Jāgaritasthāno bahiṣprajñaḥ saptāṅga ekonaviṃśatimukha
sthūlabhugvaiśvānara prathamah pādaḥ ॥3॥

जागरित Waker स्थानो state has बहिष्प्रज्ञः external awareness
सप्त seven अङ्ग mouths एकोनविंशति nineteen मुखः mouths
स्थूल physical, fat, coarse world भुक experiencer वैश्वानरः
omnipresent प्रथमः first पादः quarter

The waker state has external awareness and uses the physical
body, limbs, and sensory inputs to interact with the universe.
It is the experiencer of the physical universe, omnipresent,
and the first quarter of the self.

Mantra 4 - Self as dreamer

स्वप्नस्थानोऽन्तः प्रज्ञाः सप्ताङ्ग एकोनविंशतिमुखः प्रविविक्तभुक्तैजसो द्वितीयः पादः ॥४॥

svapnasthāno'ntaḥ prajñāḥ saptāṅga ekonaviṃśatimukhaḥ praviviktabhuktaijaso dvitīyaḥ pādaḥ ॥4॥

स्वप्न Dreamer स्थानो state has अन्तः internal प्रज्ञाः awareness सप्त seven अङ्ग limbs एकोनविंशति nineteen मुखः mouths प्रविविक्त subtle, delicate, finer world भुक्त experiencer तैजसः (is) brilliant, vigorous द्वितीयः second पादः quarter

The dreamer state has internal awareness and uses the mind, limbs, and sensory inputs to interact with the subtle universe. It is the experiencer of the subtle universe. It is brilliant, vigorous, and is the second quarter of the self.

245

Mantra 5 Self as deep-sleeper

यत्र सुप्तो न कञ्चन कामं कामयते न कञ्चन स्वप्नं पश्यति तत्सुषुप्तम्
। सुषुप्तस्थान एकीभूतः प्रज्ञानघन एवाऽऽनन्दमयो ह्यानन्दभुक्
चेतोमुखः प्राज्ञस्तृतीयः पादः ॥५॥

yatra suptona kañcana kāmaṃ kāmayatena kañcana
svapnaṃ paśyati tatsuṣuptam | suṣuptasthāna ekībhūtaḥ
prajñānaghana evā nandamayo hyānandabhuk cetomukhaḥ
prājñastṛtīyaḥ pādaḥ ॥5॥

यत्र In सुप्तो deep-sleep न no कञ्चन any कामं objects कामयते
desired न no कञ्चन any स्वप्नं dreams पश्यति visualized
तत्सुषुप्तम् । सुषुप्त deep-sleeper स्थान state एकीभूतः unified
undifferentiated प्रज्ञानघन एवा awareness mass आनन्दमयो in
bliss ही (is) indeed आनन्द bliss भुक् experiencer चेतो मुखः
doorway to experiences प्राज्ञ (is) knowledge तृतीयः third पादः
quarter

In a deep sleep, there are no objects of desire and no dreams.
The deep sleeper state is a unified and undifferentiated mass
of awareness. It holds the universe in a potential state and is
the doorway to experiences. It is knowledge and is the third
quarter of the self

Mantra 6 Deep-sleeper is a source state

एष सर्वेश्वरः एष सर्वज्ञ एषोऽन्तर्याम्येष योनिः सर्वस्य प्रभवाप्ययौ हि भूतानाम् ॥६॥

eṣa sarveśvaraḥ eṣa sarvajña eṣo'ntaryāmyeṣa yoniḥ sarvasya prabhavāpyayau hi bhūtānām ॥6॥

एष this one सर्वेश्वरः is the ruler of all एष सर्वज्ञ all knower एषोऽन्तर्याम्येष inner controller योनिः the source सर्वस्य of all प्रभव origin अप्ययौ cessation हि indeed भूतानाम् of all beings

The deep-sleeper state is the knower and controller of self. It is the source from which all beings originate and terminate.

Mantra 7 The fourth part of self

नान्तःप्रज्ञं न बहिःप्रज्ञं नोभयतःप्रज्ञं न प्रज्ञानघनं न प्रज्ञं नाप्रज्ञम् ।
अदृश्यमव्यवहार्यमग्राह्यमलक्षणमचिन्त्यमव्यपदेश्यमेकात्मप्रत्ययसा
रं प्रपञ्चोपशमं शान्तं शिवमद्वैतं चतुर्थं मन्यन्ते स आत्मा स
विज्ञेयः ॥ ७ ॥

nāntaḥprajñaṁ na bahiḥprajñaṁ nobhayataḥprajñaṁ na
prajñānaghanaṁ na prajñaṁ nāprajñam |
adṛśyamavyavahāryamagrāhyamalakṣaṇamacintyamavyapad
eśyamekātmapratyayasāraṁ prapañcopaśamaṁ śāntaṁ
śivamadvaitaṁ caturthaṁ manyante sa ātmā sa
vijñeyaḥ || 7 ||

नान्तःप्रज्ञं not conscious of the inner world न बहिःप्रज्ञं not
aware of the external world नोभयतःप्रज्ञं, not bi-directional
consciousness न प्रज्ञानघनं not a mass of consciousness न प्रज्ञं
not all-knowing नाप्रज्ञम् not unconscious | अदृश्यम Beyond
perception अव्यवहार्यम beyond transactions अग्राह्यम beyond
grasp अलक्षणम beyond inference अचिन्त्यम beyond thoughts
अव्यपदेश्यम beyond description एकात्म प्रत्यय सारं traceable
through unbroken self-awareness प्रपञ्च cosmic उपशमं
cessation/silence शान्तं peaceful शिवम auspicious अद्वैतं non-

248

dual चतुर्थं fourth मन्यन्ते considered स आत्मा that self स विज्ञेयः which needs to be realized.

This Mantra refers to that which is not just the awareness of the inner world, external world, or both worlds. It is not the consciousness, not all-knowing, not unconscious, beyond perception, beyond transactions, beyond grasp, beyond interference, beyond thoughts, beyond description. It is traceable through the unbroken self-awareness. It is satiated from the cosmos; it is peaceful, auspicious, and non-dual. This fourth part needs to be realized.

Mantra 8 Using language as a tool

सोऽयमात्माध्यक्षरमोङ्कारोऽधिमात्रं पादा मात्रा मात्राश्च पादा अकार उकारो मकार इति ॥८॥

so'yamātmādhyakṣaramonkāro'dhimātram   pādā   mātrā mātrāśca pādā akāra ukāro makāra iti ॥8॥

सः अयम अत्मा This same self अध्यक्षरम from the syllables ओङ्कार is omkar अधिमात्रं using the rhythmic and intonational aspect of language पादा subdivided into four मात्रा letters च मात्रा and the letter पादा quarters (are) अकार A उकारो U मकार M इति thus

The same self can be denoted using rhythmic and intonational aspects of language by diving Om into four parts A U M, and all of it which is Om

Mantra 9 Waker is A

जागरितस्थानो वैश्वानरोऽकारः प्रथमा मात्राऽऽप्तेरादिमत्त्वाद्वाप्नोति ह
वै सर्वान्कामानादिश्च भवति य एवं वेद ॥९॥

jāgaritasthāno   vaiśvānaro'kāraḥ   prathamā
mātrā"pterādimattvādvāpnoti ha vai sarvānkāmānādiśca
bhavati ya evaṃ veda॥9॥

जागरित स्थानो Waker's state वैश्वानर the omnipresent आकारः
A प्रथमा first मात्रा letter आप्तेः On account of its
pervasiveness वा अदिमत्त्व or being first अद्वाप्नोति ह वै indeed
attains सर्वान्कामान all desires आदि foremost च भवति and
becomes य that एवं who also वेद knows

The waking state is omnipresent and represented with the
first letter A of AUM. On account of it being first and being
everywhere, it indeed attains all that it desires and also
becomes the One who knows. In other words, this state can
also be the knower of the true Self.

Mantra 10 Dreamer is U

स्वप्नस्थानस्तैजस उकारो द्वितीया मात्रोत्कर्षादुभयत्वाद्वोत्कर्षति ह वै
ज्ञानसन्ततिं समानश्च भवति नास्याब्रह्मवित्कुले भवति य एवं वेद
॥१०॥

svapnasthānastaijasa   ukāro   dvitīyā
mātrotkarṣādubhayatvādvotkarṣati ha vai jñānasantatiṃ
samānaśca bhavati nāsyābrahmavitkule bhavati ya evaṃ
veda॥10॥

स्वप्नस्थान Dreamer's state स्तैजस the brilliant/vigorous
उकारो U द्वितीया second मात्र letter उत्कर्ष is prosperous वा or
उभयत्वा on account of being intermediate उत्कर्षत ह वै gains
excellence ज्ञान in the knowledge सन्ततिं range/scope समान
equal to all च and भवति becomes न अस्या, not in this ब्रह्मवित
ignorant of Brahma कुले lineage भवति and becomes य that
एवं who also वेद knows

The Dreamer's state is that of brilliance and is represented
by the second letter U of AUM. Due to its intermediate state
of prosperity, this state gains excellence in knowledge with a
broad range/scope. It is treated equally by all and finds no
one in his line of descendants. It is not ignorant of Brahma

and also becomes the One who knows. In other words, this state can also be self-realized.

Mantra 11 Deep-sleeper is M

सुषुप्तस्थानः प्राज्ञो मकारस्तृतीया मात्रा मितेरपीतेर्वा मिनोति ह वा इदं सर्वमपीतिश्च भवति य एवं वेद ॥ ११॥

suṣuptasthānaḥ prājño makārastṛtīyā mātrā miterapītervā minoti ha vā idaṃ sarvamapītiśca bhavati ya evaṃ veda ॥ 11 ॥

सुषुप्तस्थानः Deep-sleeper's state is प्राज्ञो awareness मकार M तृतिया third मात्रा letter मितेर measurement अपीतेर dissolution suspension मिनोति or fixed ह वा in its identity इदं सर्वम all this अपीति termination/suspension of the world च भवति and becomes य that एवं who also वेद knows.

The Deep-sleeper's state is pure awareness and is represented by the third letter M of AUM. It is a measure of dissolution and suspension of fixed identity. In this state, all the worlds are terminated or suspended. This state also becomes the one who knows. In other words, this state can also be the knower of the true Self.

अमात्रश्चतुर्थोऽव्यवहार्यः प्रपञ्चोपशमः शिवोऽद्वैत एवमोङ्कार आत्मैव संविशत्यात्मनाऽऽत्मानं य एवं वेद ॥१२॥

amātraścaturtho'vyavahāryaḥ prapañcopaśamaḥ śivo'dvaita evamoṅkāra ātmaiva saṃviśatyātmaā"tmaaṃ ya evaṃ veda ॥12॥

अमात्रः Boundless चतुर्थ fourth उव्यवहार्यः beyond transactions उप्रपञ्च beyond description उपशमः satiated शिवः auspicious अद्वैत non-dual एवम thus ओङ्कार Omkar आत्म एव self-alone संविशति rests in आत्मना self आत्मानं the self य that एवं who also वेद knows.

The fourth state is the one that is boundless, beyond transactions, beyond descriptions, fully satiated, auspicious, non-dual, and thus Omkar. It rests in itself and is also the one who knows.

Bhagwad Gita Verses Referenced

Illusion & Dualities

Verse 2:12

न त्वेवाहं जातु नासं । न त्वं नेमे जनाधिपा ।

न चैव न भविष्यामः । सर्वे वयमतः परम ॥ २-१२

na tvevāhaṁ jātu nāsaṁ na tvaṁ neme janādhipāḥ

na chaiva na bhaviṣhyāmaḥ sarve vayamataḥ param

न never एवा certainly अहम् I, जातु came to नासं not exist न
never त्वं you न never एमे all these जनाधिपा kings न never
चैव also न भविष्यामः not exist in the future | सर्वे वयम all of
us इतः परम henceforth

Never did I, you, or all these kings come into existence,
and never will there be a time when we can cease to exist.

Verse 2:13

देहिनोऽस्मिन्यथा देहे । कौमारं यौवनं जरा ।

तथा देहान्तर प्रप्तिर धीरस्त त्र न मुह्य ति ॥ २-१३

dehino'smin yathā dehe kaumāraṁ yauvanaṁ jarā

tathā dehāntara-prāptir dhīras tatra na muhyati

देहिनोS - of the embodied अस्मिन in this यथा as देहे body।
कौमारम childhood यौवनं youth जरा old age । तथा similarly

255

देहान्तर entrance in the body प्रप्तिर achieved धीरस्त त्र steadfast न not मुह्य ति perplexed

As the embodied change the body from childhood to youth and old age similarly, entrance to the body is achieved. The discerning person is not confused.

Verse 2:14

मात्रास्पर्शास्तु कौन्तेय शीतोष्णसुखदुःखदाः।

आगमा पायिनोऽनित्यास्तांस्तितिक्षस्व भारत ॥ २-१४

mātrā-sparśhās tu kaunteya śhītoṣhṇa-sukha-duḥkha-dāḥ

āgamāpāyino 'nityās tans-titikṣhasva bhārata

मात्रा only स्पर्श वास्तु physical objects कौन्तेय son of Kunti शीतोष्ण cold/heat सुखदुःखदाः joy and pain।

आगमा पायिनोऽनित्यास have a beginning and end always तमस्तितिक्षस्व endure it भारत child of India (Bharat dynasty)

All the things we physically experience in the world have a beginning and end that we must endure.

Verse 2:15

यं हि न व्यथय न्त्येते पुरुषं पुरुषर्षभ।

समदुःखसुखं धीराम सोऽमृतत्वाय कल्पते ॥ २-१५

yaṁ hi na vyathay antyete puruṣhaṁ puruṣharṣhabha

sama-duḥkha-sukhaṁ dhīraṁ so 'mṛitatvāya kalpate

यं the one who हि certainly न never व्यथय न्त्येते agitates is
पुरुषं person पुरुषर्षभ best among people। सम (endures) all
दुःखसुखं pain and joy धीराम (with) strength सोऽमृतत्वाय for
liberation कल्पते is eligible

The person who never gets agitated and endures all pain
and joy with strength is qualified for liberation

Verse 2:16

नसतो विद्यते भावो न भावो विद्यते सतः।

उभयोरपि दृष्टोऽन्तसत्चनयोस्तत्त्व दर्शिभिः ॥ २-१६

nāsato vidyate bhāvo nābhāvo vidyate sataḥ ubhayorapi
dṛiṣhṭo 'nta stvanayos tattva-darśhibhiḥ

नसतो what is untrue विद्यते there exists भावो endurance न
भावो no endurance विद्यते there exists सतः of what is true।

उभयोरपि of the two sides दृष्टोऽ observed अन्तः conclusion
तव but अनयोः of them तत्व truth दर्शिभिः by observer ॥

257

What is untrue requires endurance, and there is nothing to endure on what truly exists. The truth-seeker concludes the two sides.

Verse 2:38

सुखदुःखे समे कृत्वा लाभालाभौ जयाजयौ।

ततो युद्धाय युज्यस्व नैवं पापमवाप्सयसि ॥ २-३८

sukha-duḥkhe same kṛitvā lābhālābhau jayājayau

tato yuddhāya yujyasva naivaṁ pāpam vāpsyasi

सुखदुःखे joy & pain समे in equanimity कृत्वा having done लाभालाभौ gain & loss जयाजयौ victory & defeat।

ततो thereafter युद्धाय battle युज्यस्व for the sake of battle नैवं never पापम sins वाप्सयसि incurred ॥

Pleasure, pain gain, loss, victory defeat are to be treated equally. We need to engage in action (battle) for its sake of action and be unaffected by the results.

Verse 2:45

त्रैगुण्यविषया वेदा निस्त्रैगुण्यो भवार्जुन।

निर्द्वन्द्वो नित्यसत्त्वस्थो निर्योगक्षेम आत्मवान ॥ २-४५

trai-guṇya-viṣhayā vedā nistrai-guṇyo bhavārjuna

nirdvandvo nitya-sattva-stho niryoga-kṣhema ātmavān

त्रै य three गुण्य विषया unique attributes वेदा as per Vedas
निस्त्रैगुण्यो void of the 3 attributes भव be अर्जुन Arjuna ।

निर्द्वन्द्वो free from dualities नित्यalways सत्त्वस्थो steady in
truth निर्योगक्षेम free from the worry of acquisition or
possession आत्मवान be self-controlled/possessed ॥

There are three attributes that we need to be void of as per
the Vedas. Be free from the dualities (joy/pain, win/loss,
like/dislike, etc.) and steady in the truth (that the world is
an illusion). Be free from the worry of possessions, and
associate with the true Self - Atma.

Verse 5:10

ब्रह्मण्याधाय कर्माणि सङ्गं त्यक्त्वा करोति यः।

लिप्यते न स पापेन पद्मपत्रमिवाम्भसा॥ ५-१०

brahmaṇyādhāya karmāṇi saṅgaṁ tyaktvā karoti yaḥ |
lipyate na sa pāpena padma-patram ivāmbhasā

ब्रह्मणि Brahmani अधाय dedicating कर्माणि all activities सङ्गं
attachment त्यक्त्वा abandoning करोति performs यः who।

लिप्यते is affected न never स such a person पापेन by sins पद्मपत्रम lotus leaf इव like अम्भसा by water ॥

The Brahma-like person dedicated to all activities after abandoning attachment is unaffected by sins incurred like the lotus leaf not wet by water.

This verse explains that a supreme being immersed in work dispassionate to the outcomes is not entangled in the world. They are free, and the consequences of their selfless labor cannot burden them. Like, the lotus leaf of the aquatic plant stays in water but does not get wet.

Free from Ego

Verse 5:14

न कर्तृत्वं न कर्माणि लोकस्य सृजति प्रभुः।
न कर्मफलसंयोगं स्वभावस्तु प्रवर्तते ॥ ५-१४

na kartṛitvaṁ na karmāṇi lokasya sṛijati prabhuḥ | na karma-
phala-saṅyogaṁ svabhāvas tu pravartate

न neither कर्तृत्वं ownership न nor कर्माणि actions लोकस्य

of people सृजति creates प्रभुः the supreme |

न nor कर्मफलसंयोगं connection of fruits to action

स्वभावस्तु in accordance to nature प्रवर्तते but enacted by

nature ॥

The (supreme eternal being) does not create people's ownership or actions, nor is it responsible for connecting fruits to action. Nature enacts everything in accordance with nature.

This next verse reminds us that nature causes us to perform all kinds of activities. We are compelled by a drive or force we cannot take credit for. We are able to execute using abilities that are not ours to claim. Yet, in our ignorance, we think this is "our" achievement

261

Verse 3:27

प्रकृतेः क्रियमाणानि गुणैः कर्माणि सर्वशः।

अहङ्कारविमूढात्मा कर्ताहमिति मन्यते ॥ ३-२७

prakṛiteḥ kriyamāṇāni guṇaiḥ karmāṇi sarvaśhaḥ |
ahankāra-vimūḍhātmā kartāham iti manyate

प्रकृतेः Nature क्रियमाणानि carried out गुणैः caliber/traits/attributes कर्माणि activities सर्वशः of all kinds |

अहङ्कार ego विमूढ confused आत्मा beings कर्ता the doer अहम् । इति is मन्यते thinks ॥

Nature carries out all sorts of activities through its own attributes. The ego-centric person confuses himself as the doer.

This next verse is the polar opposite way to say exactly what 3:27 just described. Repetition is fairly frequent to make some important points stick throughout the text.

Verse 13:30

प्रकृत्यैव च कर्माणि क्रियमाणानि सर्वशः ।

यः पश्यति तथात्मानमकर्तारं स पश्यति ॥ 30॥

prakṛityaiva cha karmāṇi kriyamāṇāni sarvaśhaḥ
yaḥ paśhyati tathātmānam akartāraṁ sa paśhyati

प्रकृते: Nature ऐव truly चा also करमाणी actions

क्रियमाणानि carried out सर्वश: of all kinds।

य: who पश्यति see तथा also आत्मानम embodied self

अकर्तारम actionless स they पश्यति see॥

Only they see, who see that all actions are performed by prakruti alone, and that the Self is actionless.

Verse 3:28

तत्त्वविनु महाबाहो गुणकर्मविभागयो: ।

गुणा गुणेषु वर्तन्त इति मत्वा न सज्जते ॥ ३-२८

tattva-vit tu mahā-bāho guṇa-karma-vibhāgayoḥ | guṇā guṇeṣhu vartanta iti matvā na sajjate

तत्त्वविनु the knower of truth महाबाहो mighty-armed one

गुणकर्म (nature's) attributes of action विभागयो:

distinguish।

गुणा nature's physical capabilities गुणेषु nature's objects of perception वर्तन्त are engaged इति thus मत्वा knowing न never सज्जते gets attached ॥

The knowledgeable person, O mighty one, can identify nature's attributes of action. Knowing that nature provides the physical (body/senses) and perception (mind/intellect) capabilities, one cannot get attached to the actions (or their results).

The awakened person is constantly aware that the activities originate in the mind and belong to the mind's world. Therefore is not affected by success/failures and attachment or aversion to the results of these actions. Realizing that karma belongs to the world, we can plow through the field of activity without being attached. With this inner freedom, we can enjoy our karma with sportsmanship and be free of the compulsion to win.

Verse 2:52

यदा ते मोहकलिलं बुद्धिर्व्यतितरिष्यति ।
तदा गन्तासि निर्वेदं श्रोतव्यस्य श्रुतस्य च ॥ २-५२

yadā te moha-kalilaṁ buddhir vyatitariṣhyati

tadā gantāsi nirvedaṁ śhrotavyasya śhrutasya cha

यदा when ते your मोह attachment कलिलं (to) confusion बुद्धिर् (in your) intellect व्यतितरिष्यति has passed ।

तदा then गन्तासि निर्वेदं (you) get unattached to श्रोतव्यस्य what has been heard श्रुतस्य च what is yet to be heard ॥

When one overcomes the clinging to the confusion regarding action, one is unattached to what has been heard and what is yet to be heard (praises and/or criticism)

Verse 2:53

श्रुतिविप्रतिपन्ना ते यदा स्थास्यति निश्चला।
समाधावचला बुद्धिस्तदा योगमवाप्स्यसि ॥ २-५३

श्रुति Vedic revelation विप्रतिपन्ना in opposition (to your) belief) ते (despite that) you यदा when स्थास्यति remain निश्चला unmoved ।

समाधावचला rush towards बुद्धिस intellect तदा then योगम union with self अवाप्स्यसि is obtained ॥

Even though the Vedic revelations are in opposition to our belief, we achieve union with self(self-realization or yoga) when we remain steadfast and progress towards conceptually understanding them.

When we combine the two verses together, we get a powerful message that says - when we are not attached to our actions, meaning trying to take credit for them or sweating the win/loss, we are free from others' opinions. We do not care what is said about our work and who has heard it. We also do not care about what may be stated in the future about our efforts. We are focused on doing the best we can in the moment. It is the only sane thing to do.

Verse 2:57

यः सर्वत्रानाभिस्नेहस्तत्तत्प्रयप्या शुभाशुभम ।
नाभिनन्दति न द्वेष्टि तस्य प्रज्ञा प्रतिष्ठिता॥ २-५७

yaḥ sarvatrānabhisnehas tat tat prāpya śhubhāśhubham
nābhinandati na dveshṭi tasya prajñā pratishṭhitā

यः one who is सर्वत्रा everywhere नाभि without स्नेहस्त attachment तत्प्रयप्या is the one receiving शुभ good अशुभम, and bad ।

न without अभिनन्दति praise/applaud न not द्वेष्टि avoiding तस्य is प्रज्ञा aware/wise प्रतिष्ठिता on track ॥

The one who is everywhere without attachment and receives positive and negative without rejoicing or avoiding is wise and on the right path to self-realization.

Verse 2:58

यदा संहरते चायं कुर्मोगङ्गीनिव सर्वशः।

इन्द्रियाणिनदियार्थे भ्यस्तस्य प्रज्ञा प्रतिष्ठिता॥ २-५८

yadā sanharate chāyaṁ kūrmo 'ṅgānīva sarvaśhaḥ
indriyāṇīndriyārthebhyas tasya prajñā pratiṣhṭhitā

यदा when संहरते draw in चायं like कुर्मोगङ्गीनिव the limbs of tortoise सर्वशः all together । इन्द्रियाणिनदियार्थेभ्यस्त from the sense objects तस्य is प्रज्ञा wise, knowing प्रतिष्ठिता on track ॥

The knowledgable person on the right track withdraws from the physical senses like the tortoise draws its limbs in its shell.

Verse 2:70

आपूर्यमाणमचलप्रतिष्ठं समुद्रमापः प्रविशन्ति यद्वत्।

तद्वत्कामा यं प्रविशन्ति सर्वे स शान्तिमाप्नोति न कामकामी॥
२-७०

āpūryamāṇam   achalapratiṣhṭham   samudramāpaḥ
praviśhanti yadvat
tadvat kāmā yaṁ praviśhanti sarve sa śhāntim āpnoti na
kāma-kāmī

आपूर्यमाणम being   filled   up अचलप्रतिष्ठं
undisturbed/steady/strong समुद्रम (in the) ocean अप:
water प्रविशन्ति is absorbed यद्वत् just I
तद्वत like काम desire यं whom प्रविशन्ति is absorbed सर्वे
all स that person शान्ति peace माप्नोति attains न not
कामकामी the one following the dictates of the
passion/wishes II

The person, who can absorb all the desires like the ocean
absorbs all the water (from the rivers) pouring into it while
being steady and undisturbed, is the one who attains peace.
And not the one who follows the dictates of the desires or
passion.

Verse 2:71

विहाय कामान्य: सर्वान्पुमांश्चरति नि:स्पृह: I
निर्ममो निरहङ्कार: स शान्तिमधिगच्छति II २-७१

vihāya kāmān yaḥ sarvān pumānśh charati niḥspṛihaḥ

nirmamo nirahankāraḥ sa śhāntim adhigachchhati

विहाय giving up कामान्य: material desires सर्वान्पुमांश्चरति all the person lives नि:स्पृह: indifferent।

निर्ममो dispassionate निरहंकार: without pride/ego स with शान्ति peace अधिगच्छति attained ॥

The person who gives up material desire and lives is indifferent (to the sense pleasures), dispassionate, and lacks pride or ego attains peace.

Verse 2:72

एषा ब्राह्मी स्थिति: पार्थ नैनां प्राप्य विमुह्यति ।
स्थित्वास्यामन्तकालेऽपि ब्रह्मनिर्वाणमृच्छति ॥ २-७२

eṣhā brāhmī sthitiḥ pārtha nainaṁ prāpya vimuhyati
sthitvāsyām anta-kāle 'pi brahma-nirvāṇam ṛichchhati

एषा Such ब्राह्मी Brahmi स्थिति:state पार्थ नैनां never this प्राप्य having attained विमुह्यति is deluded ।

स्थित्वा steady/established अस्याम in this अन्तकालेऽपि even in the death-hour ब्रह्मनिर्वाणं liberation in Brahman मृच्छति attains॥

When one is steady or established in the state of Brahma, there is no more delusion (of the world). Even in the hour of death, liberation in Brahma is achieved.

Importance of Action

Verse 3:5

न हि कश्चित्क्षणमपि जातु तिष्ठत्यकर्मकृत् ।

कार्यते ह्यवश: कर्म सर्व: प्रकृतिजैर्गुणै: ॥ २-५

na hi kaśhchit kṣhaṇam api jātu tiṣhṭhatyakarma-kṛit

kāryate hyavaśhaḥ karma sarvaḥ prakṛiti-jair guṇaiḥ

न not हि certainly कश्चित् anyone क्षणम a moment अपि even जातु ever तिष्ठत्य can remain अकर्मकृत् without action ।

कार्यते are performed हि certainly अवश: helpless कर्म work सर्व: all प्रकृतिजै born of material nature गुणै: by the qualities ॥

There is no one who can remain without action even for a moment. Indeed, all beings are compelled to act by their qualities born of material nature (the three guṇas).

Verse 2:47

कर्मणे वाधिकार असतो मा फलेषु कदाचन ।

मा कर्मफलहेतुर्भूर्मा ते सङ्गोऽस्त्वकर्मणि ॥ २-४७

karmaṇy-evādhikāras te mā phaleṣhu kadāchana
mā karma-phala-hetur bhūr mā te saṅgo 'stvakarmaṇi

कर्मण्यावाधिकार असते you only have the right to action मा

never फलेषु to the fruits (of the action) कदाचन certainly

।

मा never कर्मफलहेतुर्भुर्मा act for the sake of the fruit ते

संगोऽस्त्वकर्मणि never become attached to inaction ॥

You only have the right to action and certainly never to the fruits of it. Do not act for the sake of the fruit and never become attached to inaction.

Verse 2:48

योगस्थः कुरु कर्माणि संगम त्यक्त्वा धनञ्जय।

सिद्धयसिद्धयोः समो भूत्वा समत्वं योग उच्यते ॥ २-४८

yoga-sthaḥ kuru karmāṇi saṅgaṁ tyaktvā dhanañjaya
siddhy-asiddhyoḥ samo bhūtvā samatvaṁ yoga uchyate

योगस्थः discipline of staying steadfast कुरु कर्माणि in

performance of action संगम attachment त्यक्त्वा

abandoned धनञ्जय o victor of all wealth।

सिद्धी in success असिद्धयो: in failure समो भूत्वा stay the same समत्वं योग steadiness of mind उच्यते it is called ||

Staying disciplined in abandoning any attachment while performing an action and staying the same in success and failure is called samatvam steadiness of mind.

Verse 3:9

यज्ञार्थात्कर्मणोऽन्यत्र लोकोऽयं कर्मबन्धन: |
तदर्थं कर्म कौन्तेय मुक्तसङ्ग: समाचर || ३-९

yajñārthāt karmaṇo 'nyatra loko 'yaṁ karma-bandhanaḥ
tad-arthaṁ karma kaunteya mukta-saṅgaḥ samāchara

यज्ञार्थात् for the sake of sacrifice कर्मणोs than action न्यत्र else लोको material world sयं this कर्मबन्धन: bondage through one's work |

तदर्थं that for the sake of कर्म action कौन्तेय Arjun, son of Kunti मुक्तसङ्ग:free from attachment समाचर conduct appropriately ||

Karma, done as a sacrifice for its own sake and conducted properly and dispassionately, provides freedom from bondage to the material world.

Performing every action as if it were a sacrifice (yajñā) or an offering made to the eternal force can help avoid attachments to the results.

The example often used to clarify this verse is - the Indian puja (offering) and the prasad (blessed food) received at the end of the puja. We do not perform the puja or visit a particular temple because we will get the most delicious prasad there. That would be ridiculous.

The puja is done with perfection, and whatever the conductor of the puja gives as prasad is graciously accepted by all - even if it is a food item that we do not particularly like. We put forward both our hands in a cup formation, and when the prasad is placed in our hand, we bow our heads down with gratitude. We then place the food item in our mouth and put on a smile to continue showing our acceptance and appreciation for whatever was given. Krishna says we should similarly embrace any results we get from our efforts. We need to accept the fruits of karma as the blessed food from the cosmos. It may be sweet, or it may be bitter - it is all the same to us since we did not labor for the sake of the fruit. We perform our actions to worship eternity.

Nirvana Shatakam

It is pronounced Shut-a-kum as shuta means six in Sanskrit. This mantra was composed by Sri Adi Shankaracharya, an 8th-century Vedic scholar and teacher.

It is not just the deep meaning, but when enunciated correctly, the words are very potent and create transforming vibrations within the seeker.

The poem is composed in the meter called balaka, which in Sanskrit means the bird crane. The poem's meter repeats phrases of one short and two long occurrences - na-naa-naa, thus mimicking the wing movements of a flying crane.

This poem is not merely to be understood but to be experienced.

मनोबुद्ध्यहङ्कार चित्तानि नाहं

न च श्रोत्रजिह्वे न च घ्राणनेत्रे ।

न च व्योम भूमिर्न तेजो न वायुः

चिदानन्दरूपः शिवोऽहम् शिवोऽहम् ॥१॥

I am not the mind, intellect, ego, or reflected awareness;
Not the senses that hear, smell, taste, or see;
Not space, earth, fire, or wind;
I am the eternal form of consciousness-bliss. I am Shiva!

मनो mind बुद्ध्य intellect अहङ्कार ego चित्तानि reflected conciousness only ना not अहं । न not च श्रोत्रजिह्वे just hearing or smell न च घ्राणनेत्रे not taste or sight ।

न च व्योम not the space भूर्मिर्न earth तेजो fire न वायुः nor the wind चिदा pure conciousness नन्द bliss रूपः form शिवोऽहम् I am Shiva शिवोऽहम् I am Shiva ॥ १ ॥

न च प्राणसंज्ञो न वै पञ्चवायुः

न वा सप्तधातुः न वा पञ्चकोशः ।

न वाक्पाणिपादं न चोपस्थपायु

चिदानन्दरूपः शिवोऽहम् शिवोऽहम् ॥ २ ॥

I am neither the breath nor its five components of air,
Not the seven minerals nor the five sheaths of the body,
Not organs of speech, motion, procreation, or excretion;
I am the eternal form of consciousness-bliss. I am Shiva!

न च प्राणसंज्ञो neither am I vital breath न वै पञ्चवायुः nor the five components of air न वा neither am I सप्त severn धातुः elements न वा Nor am I पञ्च five कोशः sheaths (of body) ।

न वाक्पाणिपादं Neither am I the organs of speech and movement न Nor चोपस्थपायु procreation or excretion. चिदा pure conciousness नन्द bliss रूपः form शिवोऽहम् । am Shiva शिवोऽहम् I am Shiva ॥२॥

न मे द्वेषरागौ न मे लोभमोहौ
मदो नैव मे नैव मात्सर्यभावः ।
न धर्मो न चार्थो न कामो न मोक्षः
चिदानन्दरूपः शिवोऽहम् शिवोऽहम् ॥३॥

I have no malice or desire nor greed and attachment;
I have no sense of possession nor preoccupation with vanity;
I am not bound by the pursuits of duty, acquisition, consumption, or liberation.
I am the eternal form of consciousness-bliss. I am Shiva!

न Neither मे I (am affected by) द्वेष aversion रागौ desire न nor मे I (experience) लोभ greed मोहौ or attachment मदो posessions नैव do not मे (affect) me नैव nor does मात्सर्यभावः vanity ।

न (I do not creave) धर्मो duty न nor चार्थो acquisition न

nor कामो consumption न nor मोक्षः liberation चिदा pure

conciousness नन्द bliss रूपः form शिवोऽहम् I am Shiva

शिवोऽहम् I am Shiva ॥३॥

न पुण्यं न पापं न सौख्यं न दुःखं

न मन्त्रो न तीर्थं न वेदा न यज्ञाः ।

अहं भोजनं नैव भोज्यं न भोक्ता

चिदानन्दरूपः शिवोऽहम् शिवोऽहम् ॥४॥

I am not virtue or sin, nor am I joy or sorrow;
I am not the sacred utterances, sites, scriptures, or rituals;
I am not the act of devouring, the consumed or consumer;
I am the eternal form of consciousness-bliss. I am Shiva!

न I do not want पुण्यं virtue न nor पापं sins न nor सौख्यं

happiness न nor दुःखं sorrow न nor मन्त्रो sounds

(mantras) न nor तीर्थं holy places न nor वेदा words

(Vedas) न nor यज्ञाः acts of devotion ।

अहं I am not भोजनं the act of devourment नैव not the

भोज्यं consumed न nor the भोक्ता consumer चिदा pure

conciousness नन्द bliss रूपः form शिवोऽहम् I am Shiva

शिवोऽहम् I am Shiva ॥४॥

न मृत्युर्न शङ्का न मे जातिभेदः
पिता नैव मे नैव माता न जन्मः ।
न बन्धुर्न मित्रं गुरुर्नैव शिष्यं
चिदानन्दरूपः शिवोऽहम् शिवोऽहम् ॥५॥

I do not doubt death and do differentiate based on birth.
I am not a father or mother, nor was I born,
I have no relations, no friends, no teacher, no disciples,
I am the eternal form of consciousness-bliss. I am Shiva!

न I do not मृत्युर्न शङ्का doubt death न nor do मे ।

जातिभेदः discriminate based on birthपिता नैव I am not a

father मे नैव माता nor a mother न जन्मः nor was I born

।

न बन्धुर्न I do not have any brothers मित्रं friends गुरुर्नैव

Guru शिष्यं or disciples चिदा pure conciousness नन्द bliss

रूपः form शिवोऽहम् I am Shiva शिवोऽहम् I am Shiva ॥५॥

अहं निर्विकल्पो निराकाररूपो

279

विभुत्वाच्च सर्वत्र सर्वेन्द्रियाणाम् ।

न चासङ्गतं नैव मुक्तिर्न मेयः

चिदानन्दरूपः शिवोऽहम् शिवोऽहम् ॥६॥

I am changeless and formless,
I rule over and permeate all the senses (in the body-mind),
I seek neither attachment, nor detachment, nor liberation,
I am the eternal form of consciousness-bliss. I am Shiva!'

अहं I am निर्विकल्पो changeless निराकाररूपो formless

विभुत्वाच्च I rule over सर्वत्र all सर्वेन्द्रियाणाम् senses । न

चासङ्गतं I am neither attachment नैव nor मुक्तिर्न मेयः

liberation चिदा pure conciousness नन्द bliss रूपः form

शिवोऽहम् I am Shiva शिवोऽहम् I am Shiva ॥६॥

References

APA Format Used

Aurelius, M. (121) Meditations by Marcus Aurelius Antoninus The Roman Emperor. Public Domain Book.

Bryom, T. (2001) The Heart of Awareness A translation of Ashtavakra Gita. http://www.webvertalingen.com/mediapool/110/1105679/data/The-Heart-of-Awareness.pdf

Cambridge Dictionary https://dictionary.cambridge.org/us/help/phonetics.html

Chakrabarti, Arindam (2016) Free Will and Freedom in Indian Philosophies https://www.routledgehandbooks.com/doi/10.4324/9781315758206.ch35

Chinmayananda, S. (2013) Mandukya Upanishad with Gaudapada's Karika. Central Chinmaya Mission Trust.

Csíkszentmihályi, M. (1990) Flow: The Psychology of Optimal Experience. Harper Perennial.

Eagleman D. (2011) Incognito: The Secret Lives of the Brain. Pantheon.

Easwaran, E (1999) Conquest of Mind. Penguin Books India.

Glashoff, K. (2023, June 3). Sanskrit Dictionary. https://www.learnsanskrit.cc/

Haidt, J (2006) The Happiness Hypothesis: Finding Modern Truth in Ancient Wisdom. Basic Books.

Hawking, S (2012) A Brief History of Time. Read by Michael Jackson. Phoenix Books.

Henley W.E. (1875) Invictus, Kindle Edition.

Hiemstra, G. (2019) Wisdom Library. https://www.wisdomlib.org/

Ho, M., (1989) The Implications of The Gaia Thesis: Symbiosis, Cooperativity and Coherence. https://www.i-sis.org.uk/gaia.php

Hoffman D., (2015) Consciousness and the Interface Theory of Perception. https://sites.socsci.uci.edu/~ddhoff/Chapter17Hoffman.pdf

Holt, J. (2012) Why Does the World Exist?: An Existential Detective Story. Liveright Publishing Corporation

Hume, D. (1739) Treatise of Human Nature. https://www.yorku.ca/blogan/hume_pi#

Kahneman, D. (2011) Thinking, Fast and Slow. Farrar, Straus and Giroux.

Krishnananda, S. (1977) The Brihadaranyaka Upanishad Swami Krishnananda Discourse-8 https://www.swami-krishnananda.org/brdup_audio/brdup-08.pdf

Kuhn, L. (2020) Roger Penrose - Quantum Physics of Consciousness. https://www.youtube.com/watch?v=43vuOpJY46s

Mode KARAOKE lyrics of the song Truly Madly Deeply by Savage Garden https://www.lyricsgaps.com/exercises/view/440

Mukundananda, S. (2014) Bhagavad Gita, The Song of God. https://www.holy-bhagavad-gita.org/chapter/3/verse/5

Orwell, G. (2003) Lear, Tolstoy and the Fool. https://www.george-orwell.org/Lear,_Tolstoy_and_the_Fool/0.html

Pribram, K. (1971) Languages of the Brain: Experimental Paradoxes and Principles in Neuropsychology. Brandon House.

Reese H. (2016) A Conversation With Robert Sapolsky Doesn't Believe in Free Will. (But Feel Free to Disagree.) https://www.nytimes.com/2023/10/16/science/free-will-sapolsky.html

Robinson, D. (2004) The Great Ideas of Philosophy, 2nd Edition. The Teaching Company

Sabater, V. (2021) The Phi Phenomenon: The Optical Illusion Your Brain Creates - Exploring your mind. https://exploringyourmind.com/the-phi-phenomenon-the-optical-illusion-your-brain-creates/

Sadhu Amrutjivandasji & Sadhu Achalswarupdasji [@SwaminarayanSuratSMV]. (2021, Jun 21) https://www.youtube.com/watch?v=NQhdLn7FHwA

Sarvapriyananda, S. Youtube [@VedantaNY] https://www.youtube.com/@VedantaNY

Taylor, S. (2020), An Introduction To Panspiritism: An Alternative To Materialism And Panpsychism. Zygon®, 55: 898-923. https://doi.org/10.1111/zygo.12649

The Sanskrit Channel [@TheSanskritChannel] https://www.youtube.com/@TheSanskritChannel

Vedanta Society of Southern California [@VedantaOrg] https://www.youtube.com/@VedantaOrg/videos

Young, E. (2023) An Immense World. Penguin Random House.

About the Author

Serene Rishi is a pen name for a tech professional based in Silicon Valley. She has worked in the San Francisco Bay Area for nearly 25 years at major companies like Google and Cisco and a few early-stage start-ups, where she honed her analytical rigor and structured thinking. She was born into a Muslim home, studied at a Catholic school, and married into a Hindu family.

Outside the corporate demands, the author maintains an avid interest in positive psychology, scientific theories of consciousness, and Western and Eastern philosophies. Her existential dilemmas as a modern-day professional seeking tranquility are reflected in her debut novel. She illuminates important connections between science and spiritual teachings for analytical minds seeking practical tools for enduring peace.